BY WILL DURANT

The Story of Philosophy
Transition
The Pleasures of Philosophy
Heroes of History
The Greatest Minds and Ideas of All Time

THE STORY OF CIVILIZATION

I. *Our Oriental Heritage*
II. *The Life of Greece*
III. *Caesar and Christ*
IV. *The Age of Faith*
V. *The Renaissance*
VI. *The Reformation*

ALSO BY WILL AND ARIEL DURANT

VII. *The Age of Reason Begins*
VIII. *The Age of Louis XIV*
IX. *The Age of Voltaire*
X. *Rousseau and Revolution*
XI. *The Age of Napoleon*

A Dual Biography

THE
LESSONS
OF
HISTORY

by

Will and Ariel Durant

Simon & Schuster Paperbacks

New York   London   Toronto   Sydney

Simon & Schuster Paperbacks
A Division of Simon & Schuster, Inc.
1230 Avenue of the Americas
New York, NY 10020

This Simon & Schuster trade paperback edition February 2010

SIMON & SCHUSTER PAPERBACKS and colophon are registered
trademarks of Simon & Schuster, Inc.

For information about special discounts for bulk purchases, please contact Simon
& Schuster Special Sales at 1-866-506-1949 or business@simonandschuster.com.

The Simon & Schuster Speakers Bureau can bring authors to your live event. For
more information or to book an event, contact the Simon & Schuster Speakers
Bureau at 1-866-248-3049 or visit our website at www.simonspeakers.com.

Manufactured in the United States of America

20   19   18   17   16

Library of Congress Cataloging-in-Publication Data

Durant, Will.
    Lessons of history / Will & Ariel Durant.
        p. cm.
    Originally published: 1968.
    Includes bibliographical references and index.
1. History—Philosophy. I. Durant, Ariel. II. Title.
    D16.8.D84 2010
    901—dc22   2009016081

ISBN 978-1-4391-4995-9
ISBN 978-1-4391-7019-9 (ebook)

Contents

Preface

This postlude needs little preface. After finishing *The Story of Civilization* to 1789, we reread the ten volumes with a view to issuing a revised edition that would correct many errors of omission, fact, or print. In that process we made note of events and comments that might illuminate present affairs, future probabilities, the nature of man, and the conduct of states. (The references, in the text, to various volumes of the *Story* are offered not as authorities but as instances or elucidations so come upon.) We tried to defer our conclusions until we had completed our survey of the narrative, but doubtless our preformed opinions influenced our selection of illustrative material. The following essay is the result. It repeats many ideas that we, or others before us, have already expressed; our aim is not originality but inclusiveness; we offer a survey of human experience, not a personal revelation.

Here, as so often in the past, we must gratefully acknowledge the help and counsel given us by our daughter Ethel.

WILL AND ARIEL DURANT

THE
LESSONS
OF
HISTORY

I. Hesitations

As his studies come to a close the historian faces the challenge: Of what use have your studies been? Have you found in your work only the amusement of recounting the rise and fall of nations and ideas, and retelling "sad stories of the death of kings"? Have you learned more about human nature than the man in the street can learn without so much as opening a book? Have you derived from history any illumination of our present condition, any guidance for our judgments and policies, any guard against the rebuffs of surprise or the vicissitudes of change? Have you found such regularities in the sequence of past events that you can predict the future actions of mankind or the fate of states? Is it possible that, after all, "history has no sense," [1] that it teaches us nothing, and that the immense past was only the weary rehearsal of the mistakes that the future is destined to make on a larger stage and scale?

At times we feel so, and a multitude of doubts assail our enterprise. To begin with, do we really know what the past was, what actually happened, or is history "a fable" not quite "agreed upon"? Our knowledge of any past event is always incomplete, probably inaccurate, beclouded by ambivalent evidence and biased historians, and perhaps distorted by our own patriotic or religious partisanship. "Most history is guessing, and the rest is prejudice." [2] Even the historian who thinks to rise above partiality for his country, race, creed, or class betrays his secret predilection in his choice of materials, and in the nuances of his adjectives. "The historian always oversimplifies, and hastily selects a manageable minority of facts and faces out of a crowd of souls and events whose multitudinous complexity he can never quite embrace or comprehend." [3] — Again, our conclusions from the past to the future are made more hazardous than ever by the acceleration of change. In 1909 Charles Péguy thought that "the world changed less since Jesus Christ than in the last thirty years";[4] and perhaps some young doctor of philosophy in physics would now add that his science has changed more since 1909 than in all recorded time before. Every year—sometimes, in war, every month—some new invention, method, or situation compels a fresh adjustment of behavior and ideas. — Furthermore, an element of chance, perhaps of freedom, seems to enter into the conduct of metals and men. We are no longer confident that atoms, much less organisms, will respond in the future as we think they have responded in the past. The electrons, like Cowper's God, move in mysterious ways their wonders to perform, and some quirk of character or circumstance may upset national equations, as when Alexander drank himself to death and let his new empire fall apart (323 B.C.), or as when Frederick the Great was saved from disaster by the accession of a Czar infatuated with Prussian ways (1762).

Obviously historiography cannot be a science. It can only be an industry, an art, and a philosophy—an industry by ferreting out the facts, an art by establishing a meaningful order in the chaos of materials, a philosophy by seeking perspective and enlightenment. "The present is the past rolled up for action, and the past is the present unrolled for understanding" [5]—or so we believe and hope. In philosophy we try to see the part in the light of the whole; in the "philosophy of history" we try to see this moment in the light of the past. We know that in both cases this is a counsel of perfection; total perspective is an optical illusion. We do not know the whole of man's history; there were probably many civilizations before the Sumerian or the Egyptian; we have just begun to dig! We must operate with partial knowledge, and be provisionally content with probabilities; in history, as in science and politics, relativity rules, and all formulas should be suspect. "History smiles at all attempts to force its flow into theoretical patterns or logical grooves; it plays havoc with our generalizations, breaks all our rules; history is baroque." [6] Perhaps, within these limits, we can learn enough from history to bear reality patiently, and to respect one another's delusions.

Since man is a moment in astronomic time, a transient guest of the earth, a spore of his species, a scion of his race, a composite of body, character, and mind, a member of a family and a community, a believer or doubter of a faith, a unit in an economy, perhaps a citizen in a state or a soldier in an army, we may ask under the corresponding heads—astronomy, geology, geography, biology, ethnology, psychology, morality, religion, economics, politics, and war—what history has to say about the nature, conduct, and prospects of man. It is a precarious enterprise, and only a fool would try to compress a hundred centuries into a hundred pages of hazardous conclusions. We proceed.

II. History and the Earth

Let us define history, in its troublesome duplexity, as the events or record of the past. Human history is a brief spot in space, and its first lesson is modesty. At any moment a comet may come too close to the earth and set our little globe turning topsy-turvy in a hectic course, or choke its men and fleas with fumes or heat; or a fragment of the smiling sun may slip off tangentially—as some think our planet did a few astronomic moments ago—and fall upon us in a wild embrace ending all grief and pain. We accept these possibilities in our stride, and retort to the cosmos in the words of Pascal: "When the universe has crushed him man will still be nobler than that which kills him, because he knows that he is dying, and of its victory the universe knows nothing." [7]

History is subject to geology. Every day the sea encroaches somewhere upon the land, or the land upon the sea; cities disappear under the water, and sunken cathedrals ring their melancholy bells. Mountains rise and fall in the rhythm of emergence and erosion; rivers swell and flood, or dry up, or change their course; valleys become deserts, and isthmuses become straits. To the geologic eye all the

surface of the earth is a fluid form, and man moves upon it as inse-
curely as Peter walking on the waves to Christ.

Climate no longer controls us as severely as Montesquieu and
Buckle supposed, but it limits us. Man's ingenuity often overcomes
geological handicaps: he can irrigate deserts and air-condition the
Sahara; he can level or surmount mountains and terrace the hills with
vines; he can build a floating city to cross the ocean, or gigantic birds
to navigate the sky. But a tornado can ruin in an hour the city that
took a century to build; an iceberg can overturn or bisect the floating
palace and send a thousand merrymakers gurgling to the Great Certainty. Let rain become too rare, and civilization disappears under
sand, as in Central Asia; let it fall too furiously, and civilization will
be choked with jungle, as in Central America. Let the thermal average rise by twenty degrees in our thriving zones, and we should
probably relapse into lethargic savagery. In a semitropical climate a
nation of half a billion souls may breed like ants, but enervating heat
may subject it to repeated conquest by warriors from more stimulating habitats. Generations of men establish a growing mastery over
the earth, but they are destined to become fossils in its soil.

Geography is the matrix of history, its nourishing mother and dis-
ciplining home. Its rivers, lakes, oases, and oceans draw settlers to
their shores, for water is the life of organisms and towns, and offers
inexpensive roads for transport and trade. Egypt was "the gift of the
Nile," and Mesopotamia built successive civilizations "between the
rivers" and along their effluent canals. India was the daughter of the
Indus, the Brahmaputra and the Ganges; China owed its life and sor-
rows to the great rivers that (like ourselves) often wandered from
their proper beds and fertilized the neighborhood with their over-
flow. Italy adorned the valleys of the Tiber, the Arno, and the Po.
Austria grew along the Danube, Germany along the Elbe and the

Rhine, France along the Rhone, the Loire, and the Seine. Petra and Palmyra were nourished by oases in the desert.

When the Greeks grew too numerous for their boundaries, they founded colonies along the Mediterranean ("like frogs around a pond," said Plato[8]) and along the Euxine, or Black, Sea. For two thousand years—from the battle of Salamis (480 B.C.) to the defeat of the Spanish Armada (1588)—the northern and southern shores of the Mediterranean were the rival seats of the white man's ascendancy. But in and after 1492 the voyages of Columbus and Vasco da Gama invited men to brave the oceans; the sovereignty of the Mediterranean was challenged; Genoa, Pisa, Florence, Venice declined; the Renaissance began to fade; the Atlantic nations rose, and finally spread their suzerainty over half the world. "Westward the course of empire takes its way," wrote George Berkeley about 1730. Will it continue across the Pacific, exporting European and American industrial and commercial techniques to China, as formerly to Japan? Will Oriental fertility, working with the latest Occidental technology, bring the decline of the West?

The development of the airplane will again alter the map of civilization. Trade routes will follow less and less the rivers and seas; men and goods will be flown more and more directly to their goal. Countries like England and France will lose the commercial advantage of abundant coast lines conveniently indented; countries like Russia, China, and Brazil, which were hampered by the excess of their land mass over their coasts, will cancel part of that handicap by taking to the air. Coastal cities will derive less of their wealth from the clumsy business of transferring goods from ship to train or from train to ship. When sea power finally gives place to air power in transport and war, we shall have seen one of the basic revolutions in history.

The influence of geographic factors diminishes as technology grows. The character and contour of a terrain may offer opportunities for agriculture, mining, or trade, but only the imagination and initiative of leaders, and the hardy industry of followers, can transform the possibilities into fact; and only a similar combination (as in Israel today) can make a culture take form over a thousand natural obstacles. Man, not the earth, makes civilization.

III. Biology and History

History is a fragment of biology: the life of man is a portion of the vicissitudes of organisms on land and sea. Sometimes, wandering alone in the woods on a summer day, we hear or see the movement of a hundred species of flying, leaping, creeping, crawling, burrowing things. The startled animals scurry away at our coming; the birds scatter; the fish disperse in the brook. Suddenly we perceive to what a perilous minority we belong on this impartial planet, and for a moment we feel, as these varied denizens clearly do, that we are passing interlopers in their natural habitat. Then all the chronicles and achievements of man fall humbly into the history and perspective of polymorphous life; all our economic competition, our strife for mates, our hunger and love and grief and war, are akin to the seeking, mating, striving, and suffering that hide under these fallen trees or leaves, or in the waters, or on the boughs.

Therefore the laws of biology are the fundamental lessons of history. We are subject to the processes and trials of evolution, to the struggle for existence and the survival of the fittest to survive. If some of us seem to escape the strife or the trials it is because our group protects us; but that group itself must meet the tests of survival.

So the first biological lesson of history is that life is competition. Competition is not only the life of trade, it is the trade of life— peaceful when food abounds, violent when the mouths outrun the food. Animals eat one another without qualm; civilized men consume one another by due process of law. Co-operation is real, and increases with social development, but mostly because it is a tool and form of competition; we co-operate in our group—our family, community, club, church, party, "race," or nation—in order to strengthen our group in its competition with other groups. Competing groups have the qualities of competing individuals: acquisitiveness, pugnacity, partisanship, pride. Our states, being ourselves multiplied, are what we are; they write our natures in bolder type, and do our good and evil on an elephantine scale. We are acquisitive, greedy, and pugnacious because our blood remembers millenniums through which our forebears had to chase and fight and kill in order to survive, and had to eat to their gastric capacity for fear they should not soon capture another feast. War is a nation's way of eating. It promotes co-operation because it is the ultimate form of competition. Until our states become members of a large and effectively protective group they will continue to act like individuals and families in the hunting stage.

The second biological lesson of history is that life is selection. In the competition for food or mates or power some organisms succeed and some fail. In the struggle for existence some individuals are better equipped than others to meet the tests of survival. Since Nature (here meaning total reality and its processes) has not read very carefully the American Declaration of Independence or the French Revolutionary Declaration of the Rights of Man, we are all born unfree and unequal: subject to our physical and psychological heredity, and to the customs and traditions of our group; diversely endowed in health and strength, in mental capacity and qualities of character. Nature loves difference as the necessary material of selection and evolution; identical twins differ in a hundred ways, and no two peas are alike.

Inequality is not only natural and inborn, it grows with the complexity of civilization. Hereditary inequalities breed social and artificial inequalities; every invention or discovery is made or seized by the exceptional individual, and makes the strong stronger, the weak relatively weaker, than before. Economic development specializes functions, differentiates abilities, and makes men unequally valuable to their group. If we knew our fellow men thoroughly we could select thirty per cent of them whose combined ability would equal that of all the rest. Life and history do precisely that, with a sublime injustice reminiscent of Calvin's God.

Nature smiles at the union of freedom and equality in our utopias. For freedom and equality are sworn and everlasting enemies, and when one prevails the other dies. Leave men free, and their natural inequalities will multiply almost geometrically, as in England and America in the nineteenth century under *laissez-faire*. To check the growth of inequality, liberty must be sacrificed, as in Russia after 1917. Even when repressed, inequality grows; only the man who is below the average in economic ability desires equality; those who are conscious of superior ability desire freedom; and in the end superior ability has its way. Utopias of equality are biologically doomed, and the best that the amiable philosopher can hope for is an approximate equality of legal justice and educational opportunity. A society in which all potential abilities are allowed to develop and function will have a survival advantage in the competition of groups. This competition becomes more severe as the destruction of distance intensifies the confrontation of states.

The third biological lesson of history is that life must breed. Nature has no use for organisms, variations, or groups that cannot reproduce abundantly. She has a passion for quantity as prerequisite to the selection of quality; she likes large litters, and relishes the struggle that picks the surviving few; doubtless she looks on approvingly at the upstream race of a thousand sperms to fertilize one ovum. She is more interested in the species than in the individual, and makes little difference between civilization and barbarism. She does not care that a high birth rate has usually accompanied a culturally low civilization, and a low birth rate a civilization culturally high; and she (here meaning Nature as the process of birth, variation, competition, selection, and survival) sees to it that a nation with a low birth rate shall be periodically chastened by some more virile and fertile group. Gaul survived against the Germans through the help of Roman legions in Caesar's days, and through the help of British and American legions in our time. When Rome fell the Franks rushed in from Germany and made Gaul France; if England and America should fall, France, whose population remained almost stationary through the nineteenth century, might again be overrun.

If the human brood is too numerous for the food supply, Nature has three agents for restoring the balance: famine, pestilence, and war. In a famous *Essay on Population* (1798) Thomas Malthus explained that without these periodic checks the birth rate would so far exceed the death rate that the multiplication of mouths would nullify any increase in the production of food. Though he was a clergyman and a man of good will, Malthus pointed out that the issuance of relief funds or supplies to the poor encouraged them to marry early and breed improvidently, making the problem worse. In a second

edition (1803) he advised abstention from coitus except for reproduction, but he refused to approve other methods of birth control.
Having little hope of acceptance for this counsel of sanctity, he predicted that the balance between mouths and food would be maintained in the future, as in the past, by famine, pestilence, and war.

The advances of agricultural and contraceptive technology in the
nineteenth century apparently refuted Malthus: in England, the
United States, Germany, and France the food supply kept pace with
births, and the rising standard of living deferred the age of marriage
and lowered the size of the family. The multiplication of consumers
was also a multiplication of producers: new "hands" developed new
lands to raise more food. The recent spectacle of Canada and the
United States exporting millions of bushels of wheat while avoiding
famine and pestilence at home seemed to provide a living answer to
Malthus. If existing agricultural knowledge were everywhere applied, the planet could feed twice its present population.

Malthus would answer, of course, that this solution merely
postpones the calamity. There is a limit to the fertility of the soil;
every advance in agricultural technology is sooner or later canceled
by the excess of births over deaths; and meanwhile medicine, sanita-
tion, and charity nullify selection by keeping the unfit alive to multiply their like. To which hope replies: the advances of industry, ur-
banization, education, and standards of living, in countries that now
endanger the world by their fertility, will probably have the same
effect there, in reducing the birth rate, as they have had in Europe
and North America. Until that equilibrium of production and reproduction comes it will be a counsel of humanity to disseminate the
knowledge and means of contraception. Ideally parentage should be
a privilege of health, not a by-product of sexual agitation.

Is there any evidence that birth control is dysgenic—that it lowers
the intellectual level of the nation practicing it? Presumably it has

been used more by the intelligent than by the simple, and the labors
of educators are apparently canceled in each generation by the fertility of the uninformed. But much of what we call intelligence is the
result of individual education, opportunity, and experience; and
there is no evidence that such intellectual acquirements are transmitted in the genes. Even the children of Ph.D.s must be educated
and go through their adolescent measles of errors, dogmas, and isms;
nor can we say how much potential ability and genius lurk in the
chromosomes of the harassed and handicapped poor. Biologically,
physical vitality may be, at birth, of greater value than intellectual
pedigree; Nietzsche thought that the best blood in Germany was in
peasant veins; philosophers are not the fittest material from which to
breed the race.

Family limitation played some part in the history of Greece and
Rome. It is amusing to find Julius Caesar offering (59 B.C.) rewards
to Romans who had many children, and forbidding childless women
to ride in litters or wear jewelry. Augustus renewed this campaign
some forty years later, with like futility. Birth control continued to
spread in the upper classes while immigrant stocks from the Ger-
manic North and the Greek or Semitic East replenished and altered
the population of Italy.[9] Very probably this ethnic change reduced
the ability or willingness of the inhabitants to resist governmental
incompetence and external attack.

In the United States the lower birth rate of the Anglo-Saxons has
lessened their economic and political power; and the higher birth
rate of Roman Catholic families suggests that by the year 2000 the
Roman Catholic Church will be the dominant force in national as
well as in municipal or state governments. A similar process is helping to restore Catholicism in France, Switzerland, and Germany; the
lands of Voltaire, Calvin, and Luther may soon return to the papal
fold. So the birth rate, like war, may determine the fate of theolo-

gies; just as the defeat of the Moslems at Tours (732) kept France
and Spain from replacing the Bible with the Koran, so the superior
organization, discipline, morality, fidelity, and fertility of Catholics
may cancel the Protestant Reformation and the French Enlightenment. There is no humorist like history.

IV. Race and History

There are some two billion colored people on the earth, and some nine hundred million whites. However, many palefaces were delighted when Comte Joseph-Arthur de Gobineau, in an *Essai sur l'inégalité des races humaines* (1853–55), announced that the species man is composed of distinct races inherently different (like individuals) in physical structure, mental capacity, and qualities of character; and that one race, the "Aryan," was by nature superior to all the rest.

> Everything great, noble, or fruitful in the works of man on this planet, in science, art, and civilization, derives from a single starting point, is the development of a single germ; . . . it belongs to one family alone, the different branches of which have reigned in all the civilized countries of the universe. . . . History shows that all civilization derives from the white race, that none can exist without its help, and that a society is great and brilliant only so far as it preserves the blood of the noble group that created it.[10]

Environmental advantages (argued Gobineau) cannot explain the rise of civilization, for the same kind of environment (e.g., soil-fertilizing rivers) that watered the civilizations of Egypt and the Near East produced no civilization among the Indians of North America, though they lived on fertile soil along magnificent streams. Nor do institutions make a civilization, for this has risen under a diversity, even a contrariety, of institutions, as in monarchical Egypt and "democratic" Athens. The rise, success, decline, and fall of a civilization depend upon the inherent quality of the race. The degeneration of a civilization is what the word itself indicates—a falling away from the genus, stock, or race. "Peoples degenerate only in consequence of the various mixtures of blood which they undergo." [11] Usually this comes through intermarriage of the vigorous race with those whom it has conquered. Hence the superiority of the whites in the United States and Canada (who did not intermarry with the Indians) to the whites in Latin America (who did). Only those who are themselves the product of such enfeebling mixtures talk of the equality of races, or think that "all men are brothers." [12] All strong characters and peoples are race conscious, and are instinctively averse to marriage outside their own racial group.

In 1899 Houston Stewart Chamberlain, an Englishman who had made Germany his home, published *Die Grundlagen des neunzehnten Jahrhunderts* (*The Foundations of the Nineteenth Century*), which narrowed the creative race from Aryans to Teutons: "True history begins from the moment when the German with mighty hand seizes the inheritance of antiquity." Dante's face struck Chamberlain as characteristically German; he thought he heard unmistakably German accents in St. Paul's Epistle to the Galatians; and though he was not quite sure that Christ was a German, he was confident that "whoever maintains that Christ was a Jew is either ignorant or dishonest." [18] German writers were too polite to contradict their guest: Treitschke and Bernhardi admitted that the Germans were the greatest of modern peoples; Wagner put the theory to music; Alfred Rosenberg made German blood and soil the inspiring "myth of the twentieth century"; and Adolf Hitler, on this basis, roused the Germans to slaughter a people and to undertake the conquest of Europe.

An American, Madison Grant, in *The Passing of the Great Race* (1916), confined the achievements of civilization to that branch of the Aryans which he called "Nordics"—Scandinavians, Scythians, Baltic Germans, Englishmen, and Anglo-Saxon Americans. Cooled to hardness by northern winters, one or another tribe of these fair-haired, blue-eyed "blond beasts" swept down through Russia and the Balkans into the lazy and lethargic South in a series of conquests marking the dawn of recorded history. According to Grant the "Sacae" (Scythians?) invaded India, developed Sanskrit as an "Indo-European" language, and established the caste system to prevent their deterioration through intermarriage with dark native stocks. The Cimmerians poured over the Caucasus into Persia, the Phrygians into Asia Minor, the Achaeans and Dorians into Greece and Crete, the Umbrians and Oscans into Italy. Everywhere the Nordics were adventurers, warriors, disciplinarians; they made subjects or slaves of the temperamental, unstable, and indolent "Mediterranean" peoples of the South, and they intermarried with the intermediate quiet and acquiescent "Alpine" stocks to produce the Athenians of the Periclean apogee and the Romans of the Republic. The Dorians intermarried least, and became the Spartans, a martial Nordic caste ruling "Mediterranean" helots. Intermarriage weakened and softened the Nordic stock in Attica, and led to the defeat of Athens by Sparta in the Peloponnesian War, and the subjugation of Greece by the purer Nordics of Macedonia and Republican Rome.

In another inundation of Nordics—from Scandinavia and northern Germany—Goths and Vandals conquered Imperial Rome; Angles and Saxons conquered England and gave it a new name; Franks conquered Gaul and gave it their name. Still later, the Nordic Normans conquered France, England, and Sicily. The Nordic Lombards followed their long beards into Italy, intermarried, and vitalized Milan and Florence into a Renaissance. Nordic Varangians conquered Russia, and ruled it till 1917. Nordic Englishmen colonized America and Australia, conquered India, and set their sentinels in every major Asiatic port.

In our time (Grant mourned) this Nordic race is abandoning its mastery. It lost its footing in France in 1789; as Camille Desmoulins told his café audience, the Revolution was a revolt of the indigenous Gauls ("Alpines") against the Teutonic Franks who had subjugated them under Clovis and Charlemagne. The Crusades, the Thirty Years' War, the Napoleonic Wars, the First World War depleted the Nordic stock and left it too thin to resist the higher birth rate of Alpine and Mediterranean peoples in Europe and America. By the year 2000, Grant predicted, the Nordics will have fallen from power, and with their fall Western civilization will disappear in a new barbarism welling up everywhere from within and from without. He wisely conceded that the Mediterranean "race," while inferior in bodily stamina to both the Nordics and the Alpines, has proved superior in intellectual and artistic attainments; to it must go the credit for the classic flowering of Greece and Rome; however, it may have owed much to intermarriage with Nordic blood.

Some weaknesses in the race theory are obvious. A Chinese scholar would remind us that his people created the most enduring civilization in history—statesmen, inventors, artists, poets, scientists, philosophers, saints from 2000 B.C. to our own time. A Mexican scholar could point to the lordly structures of Mayan, Aztec, and Incan cultures in pre-Columbian America. A Hindu scholar, while acknowledging "Aryan" infiltration into north India some sixteen hundred years before Christ, would recall that the black Dravidic peoples of south India produced great builders and poets of their own; the temples of Madras, Madura, and Trichinopoly are among the most impressive structures on earth. Even more startling is the towering shrine of the Khmers at Angkor Wat. History is color-blind, and can develop a civilization (in any favorable environment) under almost any skin.

Difficulties remain even if the race theory is confined to the white man. The Semites would recall the civilizations of Babylonia, Assyria, Syria, Palestine, Phoenicia, Carthage, and Islam. The Jews gave the Bible and Christianity to Europe, and much of the Koran to Mohammed. The Mohammedans could list the rulers, artists, poets, scientists, and philosophers who conquered and adorned a substantial portion of the white man's world from Baghdad to Cordova while Western Europe groped through the Dark Ages (c. 565–c. 1095).

The ancient cultures of Egypt, Greece, and Rome were evidently the product of geographical opportunity and economic and political development rather than of racial constitution, and much of their civilization had an Oriental source.[14] Greece took its arts and letters from Asia Minor, Crete, Phoenicia, and Egypt. In the second millennium B.C. Greek culture was "Mycenaean," partly derived from Crete, which had probably learned from Asia Minor. When the "Nordic" Dorians came down through the Balkans, toward 1100 B.C., they destroyed much of this proto-Greek culture; and only after an interval of several centuries did the historic Greek civilization emerge in the Sparta of "Lycurgus," the Miletus of Thales, the Ephesus of Heracleitus, the Lesbos of Sappho, the Athens of Solon. From the sixth century B.C. onward the Greeks spread their culture along the Mediterranean at Durazzo, Taranto, Crotona, Reggio Calabria, Syracuse, Naples, Nice, Monaco, Marseilles, Málaga. From the Greek cities of south Italy, and from the probably Asiatic culture of Etruria, came the civilization of ancient Rome; from Rome came the civilization of Western Europe; from Western

Europe came the civilization of North and South America. In the third and following centuries of our era various Celtic, Teutonic, or Asiatic tribes laid Italy waste and destroyed the classic cultures. The South creates the civilizations, the North conquers them, ruins them, borrows from them, spreads them: this is one summary of history.

Attempts to relate civilization to race by measuring the relation of brain to face or weight have shed little light on the problem. If the Negroes of Africa have produced no great civilization it is probably because climatic and geographical conditions frustrated them; would any of the white "races" have done better in those environments? It is remarkable how many American Negroes have risen to high places in the professions, arts, and letters in the last one hundred years despite a thousand social obstacles.

The role of race in history is rather preliminary than creative. Varied stocks, entering some locality from diverse directions at divers times, mingle their blood, traditions, and ways with one another or with the existing population, like two diverse pools of genes coming together in sexual reproduction. Such an ethnic mixture may in the course of centuries produce a new type, even a new people; so Celts, Romans, Angles, Saxons, Jutes, Danes, and Normans fused to produce Englishmen. When the new type takes form its cultural expressions are unique, and constitute a new civilization—a new physiognomy, character, language, literature, religion, morality, and art. It is not the race that makes the civilization, it is the civilization that makes the people: circumstances geographical, economic, and political create a culture, and the culture creates a human type. The Englishman does not so much make English civilization as it makes him; if he carries it wherever he goes, and dresses for dinner in Timbuktu, it is not that he is creating his civilization there anew, but that he acknowledges even there its mastery over his soul. In the long run such differences of tradition or type yield to the influence of the

environment. Northern peoples take on the characteristics of southern peoples after living for generations in the tropics, and the grand-
children of peoples coming up from the leisurely South fall into the
quicker tempo of movement and mind which they find in the North.

Viewed from this point, American civilization is still in the stage
of racial mixture. Between 1700 and 1848 white Americans north of
Florida were mainly Anglo-Saxon, and their literature was a flowering of old England on New England's soil. After 1848 the doors of
America were opened to all white stocks; a fresh racial fusion began,
which will hardly be complete for centuries to come. When, out of
this mixture, a new homogeneous type is formed, America may have
its own language (as different from English as Spanish is from Italian), its indigenous literature, its characteristic arts; already these are
visibly or raucously on their way.

"Racial" antipathies have some roots in ethnic origin, but they are
also generated, perhaps predominantly, by differences of acquired
culture—of language, dress, habits, morals, or religion. There is no
cure for such antipathies except a broadened education. A knowledge of history may teach us that civilization is a co-operative product, that nearly all peoples have contributed to it; it is our common
heritage and debt; and the civilized soul will reveal itself in treating
every man or woman, however lowly, as a representative of one of
these creative and contributory groups.

V. Character and History

Society is founded not on the ideals but on the nature of man, and the constitution of man rewrites the constitutions of states. But what is the constitution of man?

We may define human nature as the fundamental tendencies and feelings of mankind. The most basic tendencies we shall call instincts, though we recognize that much doubt has been cast upon their inborn quality. We might describe human nature through the "Table of Character Elements" given on the following page. In this analysis human beings are normally equipped by "nature" (here meaning heredity) with six positive and six negative instincts, whose function it is to preserve the individual, the family, the group, or the species. In positive personalities the positive tendencies predominate, but most individuals are armed with both sets of instincts—to meet or to avoid (according to mood or circumstance) the basic challenges or opportunities of life. Each instinct generates habits and is accompanied by feelings. Their totality is the nature of man.

But how far has human nature changed in the course of history? Theoretically there must have been some change; natural selection has presumably operated upon psychological as well as upon physio-

TABLE OF CHARACTER ELEMENTS

INSTINCTS		HABITS		FEELINGS	
Positive	Negative	Positive	Negative	Positive	Negative
Action	Sleep	Play	Rest	Buoyancy	Fatigue
		Work	Sloth	Energy	Inertia
		Curiosity	Indifference	Eagerness	Boredom
		Manipulation	Hesita-tion	Wonder	Doubt
		Thought	Dreaming	Absorption	Vacuity
		Innovation	Imitation	Resolution	Acceptance
		Art	Disorder	Aesthetic feeling	Confusion
Fight	Flight	Approach	Retreat	Courage	Anxiety
		Competition	Co-opera-tion	Rivalry	Friendliness
		Pugnacity	Timidity	Anger	Fear
		Mastery	Submission	Pride	Humility
Acquisition	Avoidance	Eating	Rejection	Hunger	Disgust
		Hoarding	Spending	Greed	Prodigality
		Property	Poverty	Possessive-ness	Insecurity
Association	Privacy	Communica-tion	Solitude	Sociability	Secretive-ness
		Seeking approval	Fearing dis-approval	Vanity	Shyness
		Generosity	Selfishness	Kindliness	Hostility
Mating	Refusal	Sexual activity	Sexual per-version	Sexual imagi-nation	Sexual neurosis
		Courtship	Blushing	Sexual love	Modesty
Parental care	Filial de-pendence	Homemaking	Filial re-bellion	Parental love	Filial re-sentment

logical variations. Nevertheless, known history shows little altera-
tion in the conduct of mankind. The Greeks of Plato's time behaved
very much like the French of modern centuries; and the Romans
behaved like the English. Means and instrumentalities change; motives and ends remain the same: to act or rest, to acquire or give, to
fight or retreat, to seek association or privacy, to mate or reject, to
offer or resent parental care. Nor does human nature alter as between
classes: by and large the poor have the same impulses as the rich,
with only less opportunity or skill to implement them. Nothing is
clearer in history than the adoption by successful rebels of the methods they were accustomed to condemn in the forces they deposed.

Evolution in man during recorded time has been social rather than
biological: it has proceeded not by heritable variations in the species,
but mostly by economic, political, intellectual, and moral innovation
transmitted to individuals and generations by imitation, custom, or
education. Custom and tradition within a group correspond to type
and heredity in the species, and to instincts in the individual; they
are ready adjustments to typical and frequently repeated situations.
New situations, however, do arise, requiring novel, unstereotyped
responses; hence development, in the higher organisms, requires a capacity for experiment and innovation—the social correlates of variation and mutation. Social evolution is an interplay of custom with
origination.

Here the initiative individual—the "great man," the "hero," the
"genius"—regains his place as a formative force in history. He is not
quite the god that Carlyle described; he grows out of his time and
land, and is the product and symbol of events as well as their agent
and voice; without some situation requiring a new response his new
ideas would be untimely and impracticable. When he is a hero of
action, the demands of his position and the exaltation of crisis develop and inflate him to such magnitude and powers as would in nor-

mal times have remained potential and untapped. But he is not merely an effect. Events take place through him as well as around him; his ideas and decisions enter vitally into the course of history. At times his eloquence, like Churchill's, may be worth a thousand regiments; his foresight in strategy and tactics, like Napoleon's, may win battles and campaigns and establish states. If he is a prophet like Mohammed, wise in the means of inspiring men, his words may raise a poor and disadvantaged people to unpremeditated ambitions and surprising power. A Pasteur, a Morse, an Edison, a Ford, a Wright, a Marx, a Lenin, a Mao Tse-tung are effects of numberless causes, and causes of endless effects.

In our table of character elements imitation is opposed to innovation, but in vital ways it co-operates with it. As submissive natures unite with masterful individuals to make the order and operation of a society, so the imitative majority follows the innovating minority, and this follows the originative individual, in adapting new responses to the demands of environment or survival. History in the large is the conflict of minorities; the majority applauds the victor and supplies the human material of social experiment.

Intellect is therefore a vital force in history, but it can also be a dissolvent and destructive power. Out of every hundred new ideas ninety-nine or more will probably be inferior to the traditional responses which they propose to replace. No one man, however brilliant or well-informed, can come in one lifetime to such fullness of understanding as to safely judge and dismiss the customs or institutions of his society, for these are the wisdom of generations after centuries of experiment in the laboratory of history. A youth boiling with hormones will wonder why he should not give full freedom to his sexual desires; and if he is unchecked by custom, morals, or laws, he may ruin his life before he matures sufficiently to understand that sex is a river of fire that must be banked and cooled by a hundred restraints if it is not to consume in chaos both the individual and the group.

So the conservative who resists change is as valuable as the radical who proposes it—perhaps as much more valuable as roots are more vital than grafts. It is good that new ideas should be heard, for the sake of the few that can be used; but it is also good that new ideas should be compelled to go through the mill of objection, opposition, and contumely; this is the trial heat which innovations must survive before being allowed to enter the human race. It is good that the old should resist the young, and that the young should prod the old; out of this tension, as out of the strife of the sexes and the classes, comes a creative tensile strength, a stimulated development, a secret and basic unity and movement of the whole.

VI. Morals and History

Morals are the rules by which a society exhorts (as laws are the rules by which it seeks to compel) its members and associations to behavior consistent with its order, security, and growth. So for sixteen centuries the Jewish enclaves in Christendom maintained their continuity and internal peace by a strict and detailed moral code, almost without help from the state and its laws.

A little knowledge of history stresses the variability of moral codes, and concludes that they are negligible because they differ in time and place, and sometimes contradict each other. A larger knowledge stresses the universality of moral codes, and concludes to their necessity.

Moral codes differ because they adjust themselves to historical and environmental conditions. If we divide economic history into three stages—hunting, agriculture, industry—we may expect that the moral code of one stage will be changed in the next. In the hunting stage a man had to be ready to chase and fight and kill. When he had caught his prey he ate to the cubic capacity of his stomach, being uncertain when he might eat again; insecurity is the mother of greed, as cruelty is the memory—if only in the blood—of a time when the

37

test of survival (as now between states) was the ability to kill. Presumably the death rate in men—so often risking their lives in the hunt—was higher than in women; some men had to take several women, and every man was expected to help women to frequent pregnancy. Pugnacity, brutality, greed, and sexual readiness were advantages in the struggle for existence. Probably every vice was once a virtue—i.e., a quality making for the survival of the individual, the family, or the group. Man's sins may be the relics of his rise rather than the stigmata of his fall.

History does not tell us just when men passed from hunting to agriculture—perhaps in the Neolithic Age, and through the discovery that grain could be sown to add to the spontaneous growth of wild wheat. We may reasonably assume that the new regime demanded new virtues, and changed some old virtues into vices. Industriousness became more vital than bravery, regularity and thrift more profitable than violence, peace more victorious than war. Children were economic assets; birth control was made immoral. On the farm the family was the unit of production under the discipline of the father and the seasons, and paternal authority had a firm economic base. Each normal son matured soon in mind and self-support; at fifteen he understood the physical tasks of life as well as he would understand them at forty; all that he needed was land, a plow, and a willing arm. So he married early, almost as soon as nature wished; he did not fret long under the restraints placed upon premarital relations by the new order of permanent settlements and homes. As for young women, chastity was indispensable, for its loss might bring unprotected motherhood. Monogamy was demanded by the approximate numerical equality of the sexes. For fifteen hundred years this agricultural moral code of continence, early marriage, divorceless monogamy, and multiple maternity maintained itself in Christian

Europe and its white colonies. It was a stern code, which produced some of the strongest characters in history.

Gradually, then rapidly and ever more widely, the Industrial Revolution changed the economic form and moral superstructure of European and American life. Men, women, and children left home and family, authority and unity, to work as individuals, individually paid, in factories built to house not men but machines. Every decade the machines multiplied and became more complex; economic maturity (the capacity to support a family) came later; children no longer were economic assets; marriage was delayed; premarital continence became more difficult to maintain. The city offered every discouragement to marriage, but it provided every stimulus and facility for sex. Women were "emancipated"—i.e., industrialized; and contraceptives enabled them to separate intercourse from pregnancy. The authority of father and mother lost its economic base through the growing individualism of industry. The rebellious youth was no longer constrained by the surveillance of the village; he could hide his sins in the protective anonymity of the city crowd. The progress of science raised the authority of the test tube over that of the crosier; the mechanization of economic production suggested mechanistic materialistic philosophies; education spread religious doubts; morality lost more and more of its supernatural supports. The old agricultural moral code began to die.

In our time, as in the times of Socrates (d. 399 B.C.) and Augustus (d. A.D. 14), war has added to the forces making for moral laxity. After the violence and social disruption of the Peloponnesian War Alcibiades felt free to flout the moral code of his ancestors, and Thrasymachus could announce that might was the only right. After the wars of Marius and Sulla, Caesar and Pompey, Antony and Octavius, "Rome was full of men who had lost their economic footing and their moral stability: soldiers who had tasted adventure and had learned to kill; citizens who had seen their savings consumed in the taxes and inflation caused by war; . . . women dizzy with freedom, multiplying divorces, abortions, and adulteries. . . . A shallow sophistication prided itself upon its pessimism and cynicism." [15] It is almost a picture of European and American cities after two world wars.

History offers some consolation by reminding us that sin has flourished in every age. Even our generation has not yet rivaled the popularity of homosexualism in ancient Greece or Rome or Renaissance Italy. "The humanists wrote about it with a kind of scholarly affection, and Ariosto judged that they were all addicted to it"; Aretino asked the Duke of Mantua to send him an attractive boy.[16] Prostitution has been perennial and universal, from the state-regulated brothels of Assyria[17] to the "night clubs" of West-European and American cities today. In the University of Wittenberg in 1544, according to Luther, "the race of girls is getting bold, and run after the fellows into their rooms and chambers and wherever they can, and offer them their free love." [18] Montaigne tells us that in his time (1533–92) obscene literature found a ready market;[19] the immorality of our stage differs in kind rather than degree from that of Restoration England; and John Cleland's *Memoirs of a Woman of Pleasure* —a veritable catena of coitus—was as popular in 1749 as in 1965.[20] We have noted the discovery of dice in the excavations near the site of Nineveh;[21] men and women have gambled in every age. In every age men have been dishonest and governments have been corrupt; probably less now than generally before. The pamphlet literature of sixteenth-century Europe "groaned with denunciations of wholesale adulteration of food and other products." [22] Man has never reconciled himself to the Ten Commandments. We have seen Voltaire's view of history as mainly "a collection of the crimes, follies, and misfortunes" of mankind,[23] and Gibbon's echo of that summary.[24]

We must remind ourselves again that history as usually written (*peccavimus*) is quite different from history as usually lived: the historian records the exceptional because it is interesting—because it is exceptional. If all those individuals who had no Boswell had found their numerically proportionate place in the pages of historians we should have a duller but juster view of the past and of man. Behind the red façade of war and politics, misfortune and poverty, adultery and divorce, murder and suicide, were millions of orderly homes, devoted marriages, men and women kindly and affectionate, troubled and happy with children. Even in recorded history we find so many instances of goodness, even of nobility, that we can forgive, though not forget, the sins. The gifts of charity have almost equaled the cruelties of battlefields and jails. How many times, even in our sketchy narratives, we have seen men helping one another—Farinelli providing for the children of Domenico Scarlatti, divers people succoring young Haydn, Conte Litta paying for Johann Christian Bach's studies at Bologna, Joseph Black advancing money repeatedly to James Watt, Puchberg patiently lending and lending to Mozart. Who will dare to write a history of human goodness?

So we cannot be sure that the moral laxity of our times is a herald of decay rather than a painful or delightful transition between a moral code that has lost its agricultural basis and another that our industrial civilization has yet to forge into social order and normality. Meanwhile history assures us that civilizations decay quite leisurely. For 250 years after moral weakening began in Greece with the Sophists, Hellenic civilization continued to produce masterpieces of literature and art. Roman morals began to "decay" soon after the conquered Greeks passed into Italy (146 B.C.), but Rome continued to have great statesmen, philosophers, poets, and artists until the death of Marcus Aurelius (A.D. 180). Politically Rome was at nadir when Caesar came (60 B.C.); yet it did not quite succumb to the barbarians till A.D. 465. May we take as long to fall as did Imperial Rome!

Perhaps discipline will be restored in our civilization through the military training required by the challenges of war. The freedom of the part varies with the security of the whole; individualism will diminish in America and England as geographical protection ceases. Sexual license may cure itself through its own excess; our unmoored children may live to see order and modesty become fashionable; clothing will be more stimulating than nudity. Meanwhile much of our moral freedom is good: it is pleasant to be relieved of theological terrors, to enjoy without qualm the pleasures that harm neither others nor ourselves, and to feel the tang of the open air upon our liberated flesh.

VII. Religion and History

Even the skeptical historian develops a humble respect for religion, since he sees it functioning, and seemingly indispensable, in every land and age. To the unhappy, the suffering, the bereaved, the old, it has brought supernatural comforts valued by millions of souls as more precious than any natural aid. It has helped parents and teachers to discipline the young. It has conferred meaning and dignity upon the lowliest existence, and through its sacraments has made for stability by transforming human covenants into solemn relationships with God. It has kept the poor (said Napoleon) from murdering the rich. For since the natural inequality of men dooms many of us to poverty or defeat, some supernatural hope may be the sole alternative to despair. Destroy that hope, and class war is intensified. Heaven and utopia are buckets in a well: when one goes down the other goes up; when religion declines Communism grows.

Religion does not seem at first to have had any connection with morals. Apparently (for we are merely guessing, or echoing Petronius, who echoed Lucretius) "it was fear that first made the gods" [25] —fear of hidden forces in the earth, rivers, oceans, trees, winds, and sky. Religion became the propitiatory worship of these forces through offerings, sacrifice, incantation, and prayer. Only when priests used these fears and rituals to support morality and law did religion become a force vital and rival to the state. It told the people that the local code of morals and laws had been dictated by the gods. It pictured the god Thoth giving laws to Menes for Egypt, the god Shamash giving Hammurabi a code for Babylonia, Yahveh giving the Ten Commandments and 613 precepts to Moses for the Jews, and the divine nymph Egeria giving Numa Pompilius laws for Rome. Pagan cults and Christian creeds proclaimed that earthly rulers were appointed and protected by the gods. Gratefully nearly ever state shared its lands and revenues with the priests.

Some recusants have doubted that religion ever promoted morality, since immorality has flourished even in ages of religious domination. Certainly sensuality, drunkenness, coarseness, greed, dishonesty, robbery, and violence existed in the Middle Ages; but probably the moral disorder born of half a millennium of barbarian invasion, war, economic devastation, and political disorganization would have been much worse without the moderating effect of the Christian ethic, priestly exhortations, saintly exemplars, and a calming, unifying ritual. The Roman Catholic Church labored to reduce slavery, family feuds, and national strife, to extend the intervals of truce and peace, and to replace trial by combat or ordeal with the judgments of established courts. It softened the penalties exacted by Roman or barbarian law, and vastly expanded the scope and organization of charity.

Though the Church served the state, it claimed to stand above all states, as morality should stand above power. It taught men that patriotism unchecked by a higher loyalty can be a tool of greed and crime. Over all the competing governments of Christendom it promulgated one moral law. Claiming divine origin and spiritual hegemony, the Church offered itself as an international court to which all rulers were to be morally responsible. The Emperor Henry IV recognized this claim by submitting to Pope Gregory VII at Canossa (1077); and a century later Innocent III raised the authority and prestige of the papacy to a height where it seemed that Gregory's ideal of a moral superstate had come to fulfillment.

The majestic dream broke under the attacks of nationalism, skepticism, and human frailty. The Church was manned with men, who often proved biased, venal, or extortionate. France grew in wealth and power, and made the papacy her political tool. Kings became strong enough to compel a pope to dissolve that Jesuit order which had so devotedly supported the popes. The Church stooped to fraud, as with pious legends, bogus relics, and dubious miracles; for centuries it profited from a mythical "Donation of Constantine" that had allegedly bequeathed Western Europe to Pope Sylvester I (r. 314-35), and from "False Decretals" (c. 842) that forged a series of documents to give a sacred antiquity to papal omnipotence.[26] More and more the hierarchy spent its energies in promoting orthodoxy rather than morality, and the Inquisition almost fatally disgraced the Church. Even while preaching peace the Church fomented religious wars in sixteenth-century France and the Thirty Years' War in seventeenth-century Germany. It played only a modest part in the outstanding advance of modern morality—the abolition of slavery. It allowed the philosophers to take the lead in the humanitarian movements that have alleviated the evils of our time.

History has justified the Church in the belief that the masses of mankind desire a religion rich in miracle, mystery, and myth. Some minor modifications have been allowed in ritual, in ecclesiastical costume, and in episcopal authority; but the Church dares not alter the doctrines that reason smiles at, for such changes would offend and disillusion the millions whose hopes have been tied to inspiring and consolatory imaginations. No reconciliation is possible between religion and philosophy except through the philosophers' recognition that they have found no substitute for the moral function of the Church, and the ecclesiastical recognition of religious and intellectual freedom.

Does history support a belief in God? If by God we mean not the creative vitality of nature but a supreme being intelligent and benevolent, the answer must be a reluctant negative. Like other departments of biology, history remains at bottom a natural selection of the fittest individuals and groups in a struggle wherein goodness receives no favors, misfortunes abound, and the final test is the ability to survive. Add to the crimes, wars, and cruelties of man the earthquakes, storms, tornadoes, pestilences, tidal waves, and other "acts of God" that periodically desolate human and animal life, and the total evidence suggests either a blind or an impartial fatality, with incidental and apparently haphazard scenes to which we subjectively ascribe order, splendor, beauty, or sublimity. If history supports any theology this would be a dualism like the Zoroastrian or Manichaean: a good spirit and an evil spirit battling for control of the universe and men's souls. These faiths and Christianity (which is essentially Manichaean) assured their followers that the good spirit would win in the end; but of this consummation history offers no guarantee. Nature and history do not agree with our conceptions of good and bad; they define good as that which survives, and bad as that which goes under; and the universe has no prejudice in favor of Christ as against Genghis Khan.

The growing awareness of man's minuscule place in the cosmos has furthered the impairment of religious belief. In Christendom we may date the beginning of the decline from Copernicus (1543). The process was slow, but by 1611 John Donne was mourning that the earth had become a mere "suburb" in the world, and that "new philosophy calls all in doubt"; and Francis Bacon, while tipping his hat occasionally to the bishops, was proclaiming science as the religion of modern emancipated man. In that generation began the "death of God" as an external deity.

So great an effect required many causes besides the spread of science and historical knowledge. First, the Protestant Reformation, which originally defended private judgment. Then the multitude of Protestant sects and conflicting theologies, each appealing to both Scriptures and reason. Then the higher criticism of the Bible, displaying that marvelous library as the imperfect work of fallible men. Then the deistic movement in England, reducing religion to a vague belief in a God hardly distinguishable from nature. Then the growing acquaintance with other religions, whose myths, many of them pre-Christian, were distressingly similar to the supposedly factual bases of one's inherited creed. Then the Protestant exposure of Catholic miracles, the deistic exposure of Biblical miracles, the general exposure of frauds, inquisitions, and massacres in the history of religion. Then the replacement of agriculture—which had stirred men to faith by the annual rebirth of life and the mystery of growth—with industry, humming daily a litany of machines, and suggesting a world machine. Add meanwhile the bold advance of skeptical scholarship, as in Bayle, and of pantheistic philosophy, as in Spinoza; the massive attack of the French Enlightenment upon Christianity; the revolt of Paris against the Church during the French Revolution. Add, in our own time, the indiscriminate slaughter of civilian populations in modern war. Finally, the awesome triumphs of scientific technology, promising man omnipotence and destruction, and challenging the divine command of the skies.

In one way Christianity lent a hand against itself by developing in many Christians a moral sense that could no longer stomach the vengeful God of the traditional theology. The idea of hell disappeared from educated thought, even from pulpit homilies. Presbyterians became ashamed of the Westminster Confession, which had pledged them to belief in a God who had created billions of men and women despite his foreknowledge that, regardless of their virtues and crimes, they were predestined to everlasting hell. Educated Christians visiting the Sistine Chapel were shocked by Michelange- lo's picture of Christ hurling offenders pell-mell into an inferno whose fires were never to be extinguished; was this the "gentle Jesus, meek and mild," who had inspired our youth? Just as the moral de- velopment of the Hellenes had weakened their belief in the quarrel- some and adulterous deities of Olympus ("A certain proportion of mankind," wrote Plato, "do not believe at all in the existence of the gods."[27]), so the development of the Christian ethic slowly eroded Christian theology. Christ destroyed Jehovah.

The replacement of Christian with secular institutions is the cul- minating and critical result of the Industrial Revolution. That states should attempt to dispense with theological supports is one of the many crucial experiments that bewilder our brains and unsettle our ways today. Laws which were once presented as the decrees of a god- given king are now frankly the confused commands of fallible men. Education, which was the sacred province of god-inspired priests, becomes the task of men and women shorn of theological robes and awe, and relying on reason and persuasion to civilize young rebels who fear only the policeman and may never learn to reason at all. Colleges once allied to churches have been captured by businessmen and scientists. The propaganda of patriotism, capitalism, or Commu- nism succeeds to the inculcation of a supernatural creed and moral code. Holydays give way to holidays. Theaters are full even on Sun- days, and even on Sundays churches are half empty. In Anglo-Saxon families religion has become a social observance and protective color- ation; in American Catholic families it flourishes; in upper- and middle-class France and Italy religion is "a secondary sexual characteristic of the female." A thousand signs proclaim that Christianity is undergoing the same decline that fell upon the old Greek religion after the coming of the Sophists and the Greek Enlightenment.

Catholicism survives because it appeals to imagination, hope, and the senses; because its mythology consoles and brightens the lives of the poor; and because the commanded fertility of the faithful slowly regains the lands lost to the Reformation. Catholicism has sacrificed the adherence of the intellectual community, and suffers increasing defections through contact with secular education and literature; but it wins converts from souls wearied with the uncertainty of reason, and from others hopeful that the Church will stem internal disorder and the Communist wave.

If another great war should devastate Western civilization, the resultant destruction of cities, the dissemination of poverty, and the disgrace of science may leave the Church, as in A.D. 476, the sole hope and guide of those who survive the cataclysm.

One lesson of history is that religion has many lives, and a habit of resurrection. How often in the past have God and religion died and been reborn! Ikhnaton used all the powers of a pharaoh to destroy the religion of Amon; within a year of Ikhnaton's death the religion of Amon was restored.[28] Atheism ran wild in the India of Buddha's youth, and Buddha himself founded a religion without a god; after his death Buddhism developed a complex theology including gods, saints, and hell.[29] Philosophy, science, and education depopulated the Hellenic pantheon, but the vacuum attracted a dozen Oriental faiths rich in resurrection myths. In 1793 Hébert and Chaumette, wrongly interpreting Voltaire, established in Paris the atheistic worship of the Goddess of Reason; a year later Robespierre, fearing chaos and inspired by Rousseau, set up the worship of the Supreme Being; in 1801 Napoleon, versed in history, signed a concordat with Pius VII, restoring the Catholic Church in France. The irreligion of eighteenth-century England disappeared under the Victorian compromise with Christianity: the state agreed to support the Anglican Church, and the educated classes would muffle their skepticism, on the tacit understanding that the Church would accept subordination to the state, and the parson would humbly serve the squire. In America the rationalism of the Founding Fathers gave place to a religious revival in the nineteenth century.

Puritanism and paganism—the repression and the expression of the senses and desires—alternate in mutual reaction in history. Generally religion and puritanism prevail in periods when the laws are feeble and morals must bear the burden of maintaining social order; skepticism and paganism (other factors being equal) progress as the rising power of law and government permits the decline of the church, the family, and morality without basically endangering the stability of the state. In our time the strength of the state has united with the several forces listed above to relax faith and morals, and to allow paganism to resume its natural sway. Probably our excesses will bring another reaction; moral disorder may generate a religious revival; atheists may again (as in France after the debacle of 1870) send their children to Catholic schools to give them the discipline of religious belief. Hear the appeal of the agnostic Renan in 1866:

> Let us enjoy the liberty of the sons of God, but let us take care lest we become accomplices in the diminution of virtue which would menace society if Christianity were to grow weak. What should we do without it? . . . If Rationalism wishes to govern the world without regard to the religious needs of the soul, the experience of the French Revolution is there to teach us the consequences of such a blunder.[30]

Does history warrant Renan's conclusion that religion is necessary to morality—that a natural ethic is too weak to withstand the savagery that lurks under civilization and emerges in our dreams, crimes, and wars? Joseph de Maistre answered: "I do not know what the heart of a rascal may be; I know what is in the heart of an honest man; it is horrible." [31] There is no significant example in history, before our time, of a society successfully maintaining moral life without the aid of religion. France, the United States, and some other nations have divorced their governments from all churches, but they have had the help of religion in keeping social order. Only a few Communist states have not merely dissociated themselves from religion but have repudiated its aid; and perhaps the apparent and provisional success of this experiment in Russia owes much to the temporary acceptance of Communism as the religion (or, as skeptics would say, the opium) of the people, replacing the church as the vendor of comfort and hope. If the socialist regime should fail in its efforts to destroy relative poverty among the masses, this new religion may lose its fervor and efficacy, and the state may wink at the restoration of supernatural beliefs as an aid in quieting discontent. "As long as there is poverty there will be gods." [32]

VIII. Economics and History

History, according to Karl Marx, is economics in action—the contest, among individuals, groups, classes, and states, for food, fuel, materials, and economic power. Political forms, religious institutions, cultural creations, are all rooted in economic realities. So the Industrial Revolution brought with it democracy, feminism, birth control, socialism, the decline of religion, the loosening of morals, the liberation of literature from dependence upon aristocratic patronage, the replacement of romanticism by realism in fiction—and the economic interpretation of history. The outstanding personalities in these movements were effects, not causes; Agamemnon, Achilles, and Hector would never have been heard of had not the Greeks sought commercial control of the Dardanelles; economic ambition, not the face of Helen "fairer than the evening air clad in the beauty of a thousand stars," launched a thousand ships on Ilium; those subtle Greeks knew how to cover naked economic truth with the fig leaf of a phrase.

Unquestionably the economic interpretation illuminates much history. The money of the Delian Confederacy built the Parthenon; the treasury of Cleopatra's Egypt revitalized the exhausted Italy of Augustus, gave Virgil an annuity and Horace a farm. The Crusades, like the wars of Rome with Persia, were attempts of the West to capture trade routes to the East; the discovery of America was a result of the failure of the Crusades. The banking house of the Medici financed the Florentine Renaissance; the trade and industry of Nuremberg made Dürer possible. The French Revolution came not because Voltaire wrote brilliant satires and Rousseau sentimental romances, but because the middle classes had risen to economic leadership, needed legislative freedom for their enterprise and trade, and itched for social acceptance and political power.

Marx did not claim that individuals were always actuated by economic interest; he was far from imagining that material considerations led to Abélard's romance, or the gospel of Buddha, or the poems of Keats. But perhaps he underestimated the role played by noneconomic incentives in the behavior of masses: by religious fervor, as in Moslem or Spanish armies; by nationalistic ardor, as in Hitler's troops or Japan's kamikazes; by the self-fertilizing fury of mobs, as in the Gordon riots of June 2–8, 1780, in London, or the massacres of September 2–7, 1792, in Paris. In such cases the motives of the (usually hidden) leaders may be economic, but the result is largely determined by the passions of the mass. In many instances political or military power was apparently the cause rather than the result of economic operations, as in the seizure of Russia by the Bolsheviks in 1917, or in the army coups that punctuate South American history. Who would claim that the Moorish conquest of Spain, or the Mongol conquest of Western Asia, or the Mogul conquest of India, was the product of economic power? In these cases the poor proved stronger than the rich; military victory gave political ascendancy, which brought economic control. The generals could write a military interpretation of history.

Allowing for these cautions, we may derive endless instruction from the economic analysis of the past. We observe that the invading barbarians found Rome weak because the agricultural population which had formerly supplied the legions with hardy and patriotic warriors fighting for land had been replaced by slaves laboring listlessly on vast farms owned by one man or a few. Today the inability of small farms to use the best machinery profitably is again forcing agriculture into large-scale production under capitalistic or communistic ownership. It was once said that "civilization is a parasite on the man with the hoe," [33] but the man with the hoe no longer exists; he is now a "hand" at the wheel of a tractor or a combine. Agriculture becomes an industry, and soon the farmer must choose between being the employee of a capitalist and being the employee of a state.

At the other end of the scale history reports that "the men who can manage men manage the men who can manage only things, and the men who can manage money manage all." [34] So the bankers, watching the trends in agriculture, industry, and trade, inviting and directing the flow of capital, putting our money doubly and trebly to work, controlling loans and interest and enterprise, running great risks to make great gains, rise to the top of the economic pyramid. From the Medici of Florence and the Fuggers of Augsburg to the Rothschilds of Paris and London and the Morgans of New York, bankers have sat in the councils of governments, financing wars and popes, and occasionally sparking a revolution. Perhaps it is one secret of their power that, having studied the fluctuations of prices, they know that history is inflationary, and that money is the last thing a wise man will hoard.

The experience of the past leaves little doubt that every economic system must sooner or later rely upon some form of the profit motive to stir individuals and groups to productivity. Substitutes like slavery, police supervision, or ideological enthusiasm prove too unproductive, too expensive, or too transient. Normally and generally men are judged by their ability to produce—except in war, when they are ranked according to their ability to destroy.

Since practical ability differs from person to person, the majority of such abilities, in nearly all societies, is gathered in a minority of men. The concentration of wealth is a natural result of this concentration of ability, and regularly recurs in history. The rate of concentration varies (other factors being equal) with the economic freedom permitted by morals and the laws. Despotism may for a time retard the concentration; democracy, allowing the most liberty, accelerates it. The relative equality of Americans before 1776 has been overwhelmed by a thousand forms of physical, mental, and economic differentiation, so that the gap between the wealthiest and the poorest is now greater than at any time since Imperial plutocratic Rome. In progressive societies the concentration may reach a point where the strength of number in the many poor rivals the strength of ability in the few rich; then the unstable equilibrium generates a critical situation, which history has diversely met by legislation redistributing wealth or by revolution distributing poverty.

In the Athens of 594 B.C., according to Plutarch, "the disparity of fortune between the rich and the poor had reached its height, so that the city seemed to be in a dangerous condition, and no other means for freeing it from disturbances . . . seemed possible but despotic power." [35] The poor, finding their status worsened with each year— the government in the hands of their masters, and the corrupt courts deciding every issue against them—began to talk of violent revolt. The rich, angry at the challenge to their property, prepared to defend themselves by force. Good sense prevailed; moderate elements secured the election of Solon, a businessman of aristocratic lineage, to the supreme archonship. He devaluated the currency, thereby easing the burden of all debtors (though he himself was a creditor); he reduced all personal debts, and ended imprisonment for debt; he can-

celed arrears for taxes and mortgage interest; he established a gradu-
ated income tax that made the rich pay at a rate twelve times that
required of the poor; he reorganized the courts on a more popular
basis; and he arranged that the sons of those who had died in war for
Athens should be brought up and educated at the government's ex-
pense. The rich protested that his measures were outright confisca-
tion; the radicals complained that he had not redivided the land; but
within a generation almost all agreed that his reforms had saved
Athens from revolution.[36]

The Roman Senate, so famous for its wisdom, adopted an uncom-
promising course when the concentration of wealth approached an
explosive point in Italy; the result was a hundred years of class and
civil war. Tiberius Gracchus, an aristocrat elected as tribune of the
people, proposed to redistribute land by limiting ownership to 333
acres per person, and alloting surplus land to the restive proletariat of
the capital. The Senate rejected his proposals as confiscatory. He ap-
pealed to the people, telling them, "You fight and die to give wealth
and luxury to others; you are called the masters of the world, but
there is not a foot of ground that you can call your own." [37] Contrary
to Roman law, he campaigned for re-election as tribune; in an
election-day riot he was slain (133 B.C.). His brother Caius, taking
up his cause, failed to prevent a renewal of violence, and ordered his
servant to kill him; the slave obeyed, and then killed himself (121
B.C.); three thousand of Caius' followers were put to death by Sena-
torial decree. Marius became the leader of the plebs, but withdrew
when the movement verged on revolution. Catiline, proposing to
abolish all debts, organized a revolutionary army of "wretched pau-
pers"; he was inundated by Cicero's angry eloquence, and died in
battle against the state (62 B.C.). Julius Caesar attempted a compromise, but was cut down by the patricians (44 B.C.) after five years of
civil war. Mark Antony confused his support of Caesar's policies

with personal ambitions and romance; Octavius defeated him at Actium, and established the "Principate" that for 210 years (30 B.C. – A.D. 180) maintained the Pax Romana between the classes as well as among the states within the Imperial frontiers.[38]

After the breakdown of political order in the Western Roman Empire (A.D. 476), centuries of destitution were followed by the slow renewal and reconcentration of wealth, partly in the hierarchy of the Catholic Church. In one aspect the Reformation was a redistribution of this wealth by the reduction of German and English payments to the Roman Church, and by the secular appropriation of ecclesiastical property and revenues. The French Revolution attempted a violent redistribution of wealth by Jacqueries in the countryside and massacres in the cities, but the chief result was a transfer of property and privilege from the aristocracy to the bourgeoisie. The government of the United States, in 1933–52 and 1960–65, followed Solon's peaceful methods, and accomplished a moderate and pacifying redistribution; perhaps someone had studied history. The upper classes in America cursed, complied, and resumed the concentration of wealth.

We conclude that the concentration of wealth is natural and inevitable, and is periodically alleviated by violent or peaceable partial redistribution. In this view all economic history is the slow heartbeat of the social organism, a vast systole and diastole of concentrating wealth and compulsive recirculation.

IX. Socialism and History

The struggle of socialism against capitalism is part of the historic rhythm in the concentration and dispersion of wealth. The capitalist, of course, has fulfilled a creative function in history: he has gathered the savings of the people into productive capital by the promise of dividends or interest; he has financed the mechanization of industry and agriculture, and the rationalization of distribution; and the result has been such a flow of goods from producer to consumer as history has never seen before. He has put the liberal gospel of liberty to his use by arguing that businessmen left relatively free from transportation tolls and legislative regulation can give the public a greater abundance of food, homes, comfort, and leisure than has ever come from industries managed by politicians, manned by governmental employees, and supposedly immune to the laws of supply and demand. In free enterprise the spur of competition and the zeal and zest of ownership arouse the productiveness and inventiveness of men; nearly every economic ability sooner or later finds its niche and reward in the shuffle of talents and the natural selection of skills; and a basic democracy rules the process insofar as most of the articles to be produced, and the services to be rendered, are determined by public demand rather than by governmental decree. Meanwhile competition compels the capitalist to exhaustive labor, and his products to ever-rising excellence.

There is much truth in such claims today, but they do not explain why history so resounds with protests and revolts against the abuses of industrial mastery, price manipulation, business chicanery, and irresponsible wealth. These abuses must be hoary with age, for there have been socialistic experiments in a dozen countries and centuries. We read that in Sumeria, about 2100 B.C.,

> the economy was organized by the state. Most of the arable land was the property of the crown; labourers received rations from the crops delivered to the royal storehouses. For the administration of this vast state economy a very differentiated hierarchy was developed, and records were kept of all deliveries and distributions of rations. Tens of thousands of clay tablets inscribed with such records were found in the capital Ur itself, in Lagash, Umma . . . Foreign trade also was carried out in the name of the central administration.[39]

In Babylonia (c. 1750 B.C.) the law code of Hammurabi fixed wages for herdsmen and artisans, and the charges to be made by physicians for operations.[40]

In Egypt under the Ptolemies (323 B.C. – 30 B.C.) the state owned the soil and managed agriculture: the peasant was told what land to till, what crops to grow; his harvest was measured and registered by government scribes, was threshed on royal threshing floors, and was conveyed by a living chain of fellaheen into the granaries of the king. The government owned the mines and appropriated the ore. It nationalized the production and sale of oil, salt, papyrus, and textiles. All commerce was controlled and regulated by the state; most retail trade was in the hands of state agents selling state-produced goods. Banking was a government monopoly, but its operation might be delegated to private firms. Taxes were laid upon every person, industry, process, product, sale, and legal document. To keep track of taxable transactions and income, the government maintained a swarm of scribes and a complex system of personal and property registration. The revenue of this system made the Ptolemaic the richest state of the time.[41] Great engineering enterprises were completed, agriculture was improved, and a large proportion of the profits went to develop and adorn the country and to finance its cultural life. About 290 B.C. the famous Museum and Library of Alexandria were founded. Science and literature flourished; at uncertain dates in this Ptolemaic era some scholars made the "Septuagint" translation of the Pentateuch into Greek. Soon, however, the pharaohs took to expensive wars, and after 246 B.C. they gave themselves to drink and venery, allowing the administration of the state and the economy to fall into the hands of rascals who ground every possible penny out of the poor. Generation after generation the government's exactions grew. Strikes increased in number and violence. In the capital, Alexandria, the populace was bribed to peace by bounties and spectacles, but it was watched by a large military force, was allowed no voice in the government, and became in the end a violent mob. Agriculture and industry decayed through lack of incentive; moral disintegration spread; and order was not restored until Octavius brought Egypt under Roman rule (30 B.C.).

Rome had its socialist interlude under Diocletian. Faced with increasing poverty and restlessness among the masses, and with imminent danger of barbarian invasion, he issued in A.D. 301 an *Edictum de pretiis*, which denounced monopolists for keeping goods from the market to raise prices, and set maximum prices and wages for all important articles and services. Extensive public works were undertaken to put the unemployed to work, and food was distributed gratis, or at reduced prices, to the poor. The government—which already owned most mines, quarries, and salt deposits—brought nearly all major industries and guilds under detailed control. "In every large town," we are told, "the state became a powerful employer, . . . standing head and shoulders above the private industrialists, who were in any case crushed by taxation." [42] When businessmen predicted ruin, Diocletian explained that the barbarians were at the gate, and that individual liberty had to be shelved until collective liberty could be made secure. The socialism of Diocletian was a war economy, made possible by fear of foreign attack. Other factors equal, internal liberty varies inversely as external danger.

The task of controlling men in economic detail proved too much for Diocletian's expanding, expensive, and corrupt bureaucracy. To support this officialdom—the army, the court, public works, and the dole—taxation rose to such heights that men lost incentive to work or earn, and an erosive contest began between lawyers finding devices to evade taxes and lawyers formulating laws to prevent evasion. Thousands of Romans, to escape the taxgatherer, fled over the frontiers to seek refuge among the barbarians. Seeking to check this elusive mobility, and to facilitate regulation and taxation, the government issued decrees binding the peasant to his field and the worker to his shop until all his debts and taxes had been paid. In this and other ways medieval serfdom began. [43]

China has had several attempts at state socialism. Szuma Ch'ien (b. c.145 B.C.) informs us that to prevent private individuals from "reserving to their sole use the riches of the mountains and the sea in order to gain a fortune, and from putting the lower classes into subjection to themselves," [44] the Emperor Wu Ti (r. 140 B.C. – 87 B.C.) nationalized the resources of the soil, extended governmental direction over transport and trade, laid a tax upon incomes, and established public works, including canals that bound the rivers together and irrigated the fields. The state accumulated stockpiles of goods, sold these when prices were rising, bought more when prices were falling; thus, says Szuma Ch'ien, "the rich merchants and large shopkeepers would be prevented from making big profits, . . . and prices would be regulated in the Empire." [45] For a time, we are told, China prospered as never before. A combination of "acts of God" with human deviltry put an end to the experiment after the death of the Emperor. Floods alternated with droughts, created tragic shortages, and raised prices beyond control. Businessmen protested that taxes were making them support the lazy and the incompetent. Harassed by the high cost of living, the poor joined the rich in clamoring for a return to the old ways, and some proposed that the inventor of the new system be boiled alive. The reforms were one by one rescinded, and were almost forgotten when they were revived by a Chinese philosopher-king.

Wang Mang (r. A.D. 9–23) was an accomplished scholar, a patron of literature, a millionaire who scattered his riches among his friends and the poor. Having seized the throne, he surrounded himself with men trained in letters, science, and philosophy. He nationalized the land, divided it into equal tracts among the peasants, and put an end to slavery. Like Wu Ti, he tried to control prices by the accumulation or release of stockpiles. He made loans at low interest to private enterprise. The groups whose profits had been clipped by his legislation united to plot his fall; they were helped by drought and flood and foreign invasion. The rich Liu family put itself at the head of a general rebellion, slew Wang Mang, and repealed his legislation. Everything was as before. [46]

A thousand years later Wang An-shih, as premier (1068–85), undertook a pervasive governmental domination of the Chinese economy. "The state," he held, "should take the entire management of commerce, industry, and agriculture into its own hands, with a view to succoring the working classes and preventing them from being ground into the dust by the rich." [47] He rescued the peasants from the moneylenders by loans at low interest. He encouraged new settlers by advancing them seed and other aid, to be repaid out of the later yield of their land. He organized great engineering works to control floods and check unemployment. Boards were appointed in every district to regulate wages and prices. Commerce was national-ized. Pensions were provided for the aged, the unemployed, and the poor. Education and the examination system (by which admission to governmental office was determined) were reformed; "pupils threw away their textbooks of rhetoric," says a Chinese historian, "and be-gan to study primers of history, geography, and political econ-omy." [48]

What undermined the experiment? First, high taxes, laid upon all to finance a swelling band of governmental employees. Second, con-scription of a male in every family to man the armies made necessary by barbarian invasions. Third, corruption in the bureaucracy; China, like other nations, was faced with a choice between private plunder and public graft. Conservatives, led by Wang An-shih's brother, ar-gued that human corruptibility and incompetence make governmen-tal control of industry impracticable, and that the best economy is a *laissez-faire* system that relies on the natural impulses of men. The rich, stung by the high taxation of their fortunes and the monopoly of commerce by the government, poured out their resources in a campaign to discredit the new system, to obstruct its enforcement, and to bring it to an end. This movement, well organized, exerted constant pressure upon the Emperor. When another period of drought and flood was capped by the appearance of a terrifying comet, the Son of Heaven dismissed Wang An-shih, revoked his de-crees, and called the opposition to power.[49]

The longest-lasting regime of socialism yet known to history was set up by the Incas in what we now call Peru, at some time in the thirteenth century. Basing their power largely on popular belief that the earthly sovereign was the delegate of the Sun God, the Incas organized and directed all agriculture, labor, and trade. A governmental census kept account of materials, individuals, and income; professional "runners," using a remarkable system of roads, maintained the network of communication indispensable to such detailed rule over so large a territory. Every person was an employee of the state, and seems to have accepted this condition cheerfully as a promise of security and food. This system endured till the conquest of Peru by Pizarro in 1533.

On the opposite slope of South America, in a Portuguese colony along the Uruguay River, 150 Jesuits organized 200,000 Indians into another socialistic society (c. 1620–1750). The ruling priests managed nearly all agriculture, commerce, and industry. They allowed each youth to choose among the trades they taught, but they required every able-bodied person to work eight hours a day. They provided for recreation, arranged sports, dances, and choral performances of a thousand voices, and trained orchestras that played European music. They served also as teachers, physicians, and judges, and devised a penal code that excluded capital punishment. By all accounts the natives were docile and content, and when the community was attacked it defended itself with an ardor and ability that surprised the assailants. In 1750 Portugal ceded to Spain territory including seven of the Jesuit settlements. A rumor having spread that the lands of these colonies contained gold, the Spanish in America insisted on immediate occupation; the Portuguese government under Pombal (then at odds with the Jesuits) ordered the priests and the natives to leave the settlements; and after some resistance by the Indians the experiment came to an end.[50]

In the social revolt that accompanied the Protestant Reformation in Germany, communistic slogans based on the Bible were advanced by several rebel leaders. Thomas Münzer, a preacher, called upon the people to overthrow the princes, the clergy, and the capitalists, and to establish a "refined society" in which all things were to be in common.[51] He recruited an army of peasants, inspired them with accounts of communism among the Apostles, and led them to battle. They were defeated, five thousand of them were slain, Münzer was beheaded (1525). Hans Hut, accepting Münzer's teachings, organized at Austerlitz an Anabaptist community that practiced communism for almost a century (c. 1530–1622). John of Leiden led a group of Anabaptists in capturing control of Münster, the capital of Westphalia; there, for fourteen months, they maintained a communistic regime (1534–35).[52]

In the seventeenth century a group of "Levellers" in Cromwell's army begged him in vain to establish a communistic utopia in England. The socialist agitation subsided during the Restoration, but it rose again when the Industrial Revolution revealed the greed and brutality of early capitalism—child labor, woman labor, long hours, low wages, and disease-breeding factories and slums. Karl Marx and Friedrich Engels gave the movement its Magna Carta in the *Communist Manifesto* of 1847, and its Bible in *Das Kapital* (1867–95). They expected that socialism would be effected first in England, because industry was there most developed and had reached a stage of centralized management that seemed to invite appropriation by the government. They did not live long enough to be surprised by the outbreak of Communism in Russia.

Why did modern socialism come first in a Russia where capitalism was in its infancy and there were no large corporations to ease the transition to state control? Centuries of peasant poverty and reams of intellectual revolt had prepared the way, but the peasants had been freed from serfdom in 1861, and the intellectuals had been inclined toward an anarchism antipodal to an all-absorbing state. Probably the

Russian Revolution of 1917 succeeded because the Czarist government had been defeated and disgraced by war and bad management;
the Russian economy had collapsed in chaos, the peasants returned
from the front carrying arms, and Lenin and Trotsky had been given
safe conduct and bon voyage by the German government. The Revolution took a Communistic form because the new state was challenged by internal disorder and external attack; the people reacted as
any nation will react under siege—it put aside all individual freedom
until order and security could be restored. Here too Communism
was a war economy. Perhaps it survives through continued fear of
war; given a generation of peace it would presumably be eroded by
the nature of man.

Socialism in Russia is now restoring individualistic motives to give
its system greater productive stimulus, and to allow its people more
physical and intellectual liberty. Meanwhile capitalism undergoes a
correlative process of limiting individualistic acquisition by semi-
socialistic legislation and the redistribution of wealth through the
"welfare state." Marx was an unfaithful disciple of Hegel: he inter-
preted the Hegelian dialectic as implying that the struggle between
capitalism and socialism would end in the complete victory of socialism; but if the Hegelian formula of thesis, antithesis, and synthesis is
applied to the Industrial Revolution as thesis, and to capitalism versus
socialism as antithesis, the third condition would be a synthesis of
capitalism and socialism; and to this reconciliation the Western
world visibly moves. Year by year the role of Western governments
in the economy rises, the share of the private sector declines. Capitalism retains the stimulus of private property, free enterprise, and
competition, and produces a rich supply of goods; high taxation,
falling heavily upon the upper classes, enables the government to
provide for a self-limited population unprecedented services in edu-

cation, health, and recreation. The fear of capitalism has compelled socialism to widen freedom, and the fear of socialism has compelled capitalism to increase equality. East is West and West is East, and soon the twain will meet.

X. Government and History

Alexander Pope thought that only a fool would dispute over forms of government. History has a good word to say for all of them, and for government in general. Since men love freedom, and the freedom of individuals in society requires some regulation of conduct, the first condition of freedom is its limitation; make it absolute and it dies in chaos. So the prime task of government is to establish order; organized central force is the sole alternative to incalculable and disruptive force in private hands. Power naturally converges to a center, for it is ineffective when divided, diluted, and spread, as in Poland under the *liberum veto*; hence, the centralization of power in the monarchy by Richelieu or Bismarck, over the protest of feudal barons, has been praised by historians. A similar process has centered power in the federal government in the United States; it was of no use to talk of "states' rights" when the economy was ignoring state boundaries and could be regulated only by some central authority. Today international government is developing as industry, commerce, and finance override frontiers and take international forms.

Monarchy seems to be the most natural kind of government, since it applies to the group the authority of the father in a family or of the chieftain in a warrior band. If we were to judge forms of government from their prevalence and duration in history we should have to give the palm to monarchy; democracies, by contrast, have been hectic interludes.

After the breakdown of Roman democracy in the class wars of the Gracchi, Marius, and Caesar, Augustus organized, under what in effect was monarchical rule, the greatest achievement in the history of statesmanship—that Pax Romana which maintained peace from 30 B.C. to A.D. 180 throughout an empire ranging from the Atlantic to the Euphrates and from Scotland to the Black Sea. After him monarchy disgraced itself under Caligula, Nero, and Domitian; but after them came Nerva, Trajan, Hadrian, Antoninus Pius, and Marcus Aurelius—"the finest succession of good and great sovereigns," Renan called them, "that the world has ever had." [53] "If," said Gibbon, "a man were called upon to fix the period during which the condition of the human race was most happy and prosperous, he would without hesitation name that which elapsed from the accession of Nerva to the death of Marcus Aurelius. Their united reigns are possibly the only period of history in which the happiness of a great people was the sole object of government." [54] In that brilliant age, when Rome's subjects complimented themselves on being under her rule, monarchy was adoptive: the emperor transmitted his authority not to his offspring but to the ablest man he could find; he adopted this man as his son, trained him in the functions of government, and gradually surrendered to him the reins of power. The system worked well, partly because neither Trajan nor Hadrian had a son, and the sons of Antoninus Pius died in childhood. Marcus Aurelius had a son, Commodus, who succeeded him because the philosopher failed to name another heir; soon chaos was king.*

---

* We should add that some historians consider the age of the Antonines as an unsuccessful "rally" in the decay of Rome. See Arnold J. Toynbee, *A Study of History* (London, 1934 f.), IV, 60.

All in all, monarchy has had a middling record. Its wars of succession brought mankind as much evil as the continuity or "legitimacy" of the monarchy brought good. When it is hereditary it is likely to be more prolific of stupidity, nepotism, irresponsibility, and extravagance than of nobility or statesmanship. Louis XIV has often been taken as the paragon of modern monarchs, but the people of France rejoiced at his death. The complexity of contemporary states seems to break down any single mind that tries to master it.

Hence most governments have been oligarchies—ruled by a minority, chosen either by birth, as in aristocracies, or by a religious organization, as in theocracies, or by wealth, as in democracies. It is unnatural (as even Rousseau saw) for a majority to rule, for a majority can seldom be organized for united and specific action, and a minority can. If the majority of abilities is contained in a minority of men, minority government is as inevitable as the concentration of wealth; the majority can do no more than periodically throw out one minority and set up another. The aristocrat holds that political selection by birth is the sanest alternative to selection by money or theology or violence. Aristocracy withdraws a few men from the exhausting and coarsening strife of economic competition, and trains them from birth, through example, surroundings, and minor office, for the tasks of government; these tasks require a special preparation that no ordinary family or background can provide. Aristocracy is not only a nursery of statesmanship, it is also a repository and vehicle of culture, manners, standards, and tastes, and serves thereby as a stabilizing barrier to social fads, artistic crazes, or neurotically rapid changes in the moral code. See what has happened to morals, manners, style, and art since the French Revolution.

Aristocracies have inspired, supported, and controlled art, but they have rarely produced it. The aristocrat looks upon artists as manual laborers; he prefers the art of life to the life of art, and would never think of reducing himself to the consuming toil that is usually the price of genius. He does not often produce literature, for he thinks of writing for publication as exhibitionism and salesmanship. The result has been, in modern aristocracies, a careless and dilettante hedonism, a lifelong holiday in which the privileges of place were enjoyed to the full, and the responsibilities were often ignored. Hence the decay of some aristocracies. Only three generations intervened between *"L'état c'est moi"* and *"Après moi le déluge."*

So the services of aristocracy did not save it when it monopolized privilege and power too narrowly, when it oppressed the people with selfish and myopic exploitation, when it retarded the growth of the nation by a blind addiction to ancestral ways, when it consumed the men and resources of the state in the lordly sport of dynastic or territorial wars. Then the excluded banded together in wild revolt; the new rich combined with the poor against obstruction and stagnation; the guillotine cut off a thousand noble heads; and democracy took its turn in the misgovernment of mankind.

Does history justify revolutions? This is an old debate, well illustrated by Luther's bold break from the Catholic Church versus Erasmus' plea for patient and orderly reform, or by Charles James Fox's stand for the French Revolution versus Edmund Burke's defense of "prescription" and continuity. In some cases outworn and inflexible institutions seem to require violent overthrow, as in Russia in 1917. But in most instances the effects achieved by the revolution would apparently have come without it through the gradual compulsion of economic developments. America would have become the dominant factor in the English-speaking world without any revolution. The French Revolution replaced the landowning aristocracy with the money-controlling business class as the ruling power; but a similar result occurred in nineteenth-century England without bloodshed, and without disturbing the public peace. To break sharply with the past is to court the madness that may follow the shock of sudden blows or mutilations. As the sanity of the individual lies in the continuity of his memories, so the sanity of a group lies in the continuity of its traditions; in either case a break in the chain invites a neurotic reaction, as in the Paris massacres of September, 1792.*

Since wealth is an order and procedure of production and exchange rather than an accumulation of (mostly perishable) goods, and is a trust (the "credit system") in men and institutions rather than in the intrinsic value of paper money or checks, violent revolutions do not so much redistribute wealth as destroy it. There may be a redivision of the land, but the natural inequality of men soon re-creates an inequality of possessions and privileges, and raises to power a new minority with essentially the same instincts as in the old. The only real revolution is in the enlightenment of the mind and the improvement of character, the only real emancipation is individual, and the only real revolutionists are philosophers and saints.

In strict usage of the term, democracy has existed only in modern times, for the most part since the French Revolution. As male adult suffrage in the United States it began under Andrew Jackson; as adult suffrage it began in our youth. In ancient Attica, out of a total population of 315,000 souls, 115,000 were slaves, and only 43,000 were citizens with the right to vote.[55] Women, nearly all workingmen, nearly all shopkeepers and tradesmen, and all resident aliens were excluded from the franchise. The citizen minority was divided into two factions: the oligarchic—chiefly the landed aristocracy and the upper bourgeoisie; and the democratic—small landowners and

---

*See Taine's unforgettable description in *The French Revolution* (New York, 1931), II, 209–33.

small businessmen, and citizens who had lapsed into wage labor but still retained the franchise. During the ascendancy of Pericles (460–430 B.C.) the aristocracy prevailed, and Athens had her supreme age in literature, drama, and art. After his death, and the disgrace of the aristocracy through the defeat of Athens in the Peloponnesian War (431–404 B.C.), the *demos*, or lower class of citizens, rose to power, much to the disgust of Socrates and Plato. From Solon to the Roman conquest of Greece (146 B.C.) the conflict of oligarchs and democrats was waged with books, plays, orations, votes, ostracism, assassination, and civil war. At Corcyra (now Corfu), in 427 B.C., the ruling oligarchy assassinated sixty leaders of the popular party; the democrats overturned the oligarchs, tried fifty of them before a kind of Committee of Public Safety, executed all fifty, and starved hundreds of aristocratic prisoners to death. Thucydides' description reminds us of Paris in 1792–93.

> During seven days the Corcyreans were engaged in butchering those of their fellow citizens whom they regarded as their enemies. . . . Death raged in every shape, and, as usually happens at such times, there was no length to which violence did not go; sons were killed by their fathers, and suppliants were dragged from the altar or slain on it. . . . Revolution thus ran its course from city to city, and the places where it arrived last, from having heard what had been done before, carried to a still greater excess the . . . atrocity of their reprisals. . . . Corcyra gave the first example of these crimes, . . . of the revenge exacted by the governed (who had never experienced equitable treatment, or, indeed, aught but violence, from their rulers) and . . . of the savage and pitiless excesses into which men were hurried by their passions. . . . Meanwhile the moderate part of the citizens perished between the two [warring groups]. . . . The whole Hellenic world was convulsed.[56]

In his *Republic* Plato made his mouthpiece, Socrates, condemn the triumphant democracy of Athens as a chaos of class violence, cultural decadence, and moral degeneration. The democrats contemptuously rejected temperance as unmanliness. . . . Insolence they term breeding, and anarchy liberty, and waste magnificence, and impudence courage. . . . The father gets accustomed to descend to the level of his sons and to fear them, and the son to be on a level with his father, having no shame or fear of his parents. . . . The teacher fears and flatters his scholars, and the scholars despise their masters and tutors. . . . The old do not like to be thought morose and authoritative, and therefore they imitate the young. . . . Nor must I forget to tell of the liberty and equality of the two sexes in relation to each other. . . . The citizens chafe impatiently at the least touch of authority, and at length . . . they cease to care even for the laws, written or unwritten. . . . And this is the fair and glorious beginning out of which springs dictatorship [*tyrannis*]. . . . The excessive increase of anything causes a reaction in the opposite direction; . . . dictatorship naturally arises out of democracy, and the most aggravated form of tyranny and slavery out of the most extreme form of liberty.[57]

By the time of Plato's death (347 B.C.) his hostile analysis of Athenian democracy was approaching apparent confirmation by history. Athens recovered wealth, but this was now commercial rather than landed wealth; industrialists, merchants, and bankers were at the top of the reshuffled heap. The change produced a feverish struggle for money, a *pleonexia*, as the Greeks called it—an appetite for more and more. The *nouveaux riches* (*neoplutoi*) built gaudy mansions, bedecked their women with costly robes and jewelry, spoiled them with dozens of servants, rivaled one another in the feasts with which they regaled their guests. The gap between the rich and the poor widened; Athens was divided, as Plato put it, into "two cities: . . . one the city of the poor, the other of the rich, the one at war with the other." [58] The poor schemed to despoil the rich by legislation, taxation, and revolution; the rich organized themselves for protection against the poor. The members of some oligarchic organizations, says Aristotle, took a solemn oath: "I will be an adversary of the people" (i.e., the commonalty), "and in the Council I will do it all the evil that I can." [59] "The rich have become so unsocial," wrote Isocrates about 366 B.C., "that those who own property had rather throw their possessions into the sea than lend aid to the needy, while those who are in poorer circumstances would less gladly find a treasure than seize the possessions of the rich." [60] The poorer citizens captured control of the Assembly, and began to vote the money of the rich into the coffers of the state, for redistribution among the people through governmental enterprises and subsidies. The politicians strained their ingenuity to discover new sources of public revenue. In some cities the decentralizing of wealth was more direct: the debtors in Mytilene massacred their creditors en masse; the democrats of Argos fell upon the rich, killed hundreds of them, and confiscated their property. The moneyed families of otherwise hostile Greek states leagued themselves secretly for mutual aid against popular revolts. The middle classes, as well as the rich, began to distrust democracy as empowered envy, and the poor distrusted it as a sham equality of votes nullified by a gaping inequality of wealth. The rising bitterness of the class war left Greece internally as well as internationally divided when Philip of Macedon pounced down upon it in 338 B.C., and many rich Greeks welcomed his coming as preferable to revolution. Athenian democracy disappeared under Macedonian dictatorship.[61]

Plato's reduction of political evolution to a sequence of monarchy, aristocracy, democracy, and dictatorship found another illustration in the history of Rome. During the third and second centuries before Christ a Roman oligarchy organized a foreign policy and a disciplined army, and conquered and exploited the Mediterranean world. The wealth so won was absorbed by the patricians, and the commerce so developed raised to luxurious opulence the upper middle class.

Conquered Greeks, Orientals, and Africans were brought to Italy to serve as slaves on the *latifundia;* the native farmers, displaced from the soil, joined the restless, breeding proletariat in the cities, to enjoy the monthly dole of grain that Caius Gracchus had secured for the poor in 123 B.C. Generals and proconsuls returned from the provinces loaded with spoils for themselves and the ruling class; millionaires multiplied; mobile money replaced land as the source or instrument of political power; rival factions competed in the wholesale purchase of candidates and votes; in 53 B.C. one group of voters received ten million sesterces for its support.[62] When money failed, murder was available: citizens who had voted the wrong way were in some instances beaten close to death and their houses were set on fire. Antiquity had never known so rich, so powerful, and so corrupt a government.[63] The aristocrats engaged Pompey to maintain their ascendancy; the commoners cast in their lot with Caesar; ordeal of battle replaced the auctioning of victory; Caesar won, and established a popular dictatorship. Aristocrats killed him, but ended by accepting the dictatorship of his grandnephew and stepson Augustus (27 B.C.). Democracy ended, monarchy was restored; the Platonic wheel had come full turn.

We may infer, from these classic examples, that ancient democracy, corroded with slavery, venality, and war, did not deserve the name, and offers no fair test of popular government. In America democracy had a wider base. It began with the advantage of a British heritage: Anglo-Saxon law, which, from Magna Carta onward, had defended the citizens against the state; and Protestantism, which had opened the way to religious and mental liberty. The American Revolution was not only a revolt of colonials against a distant government; it was also an uprising of a native middle class against an imported aristocracy. The rebellion was eased and quickened by an abundance of free land and a minimum of legislation. Men who owned the soil they tilled, and (within the limits of nature) controlled the conditions under which they lived, had an economic footing for political freedom; their personality and character were rooted in the earth. It was such men who made Jefferson president—Jefferson who was as skeptical as Voltaire and as revolutionary as Rousseau. A government that governed least was admirably suited to liberate those individualistic energies that transformed America from a wilderness to a material utopia, and from the child and ward to the rival and guardian of Western Europe. And while rural isolation enhanced the freedom of the individual, national isolation provided liberty and security within protective seas. These and a hundred other conditions gave to America a democracy more basic and universal than history had ever seen.

Many of these formative conditions have disappeared. Personal isolation is gone through the growth of cities. Personal independence is gone through the dependence of the worker upon tools and capital that he does not own, and upon conditions that he cannot control. War becomes more consuming, and the individual is helpless to understand its causes or to escape its effects. Free land is gone, though home ownership spreads—with a minimum of land. The once self-employed shopkeeper is in the toils of the big distributor, and may echo Marx's complaint that everything is in chains. Economic freedom, even in the middle classes, becomes more and more exceptional, making political freedom a consolatory pretense. And all this has come about not (as we thought in our hot youth) through the perversity of the rich, but through the impersonal fatality of economic development, and through the nature of man. Every advance in the complexity of the economy puts an added premium upon superior ability, and intensifies the concentration of wealth, responsibility, and political power.

Democracy is the most difficult of all forms of government, since it requires the widest spread of intelligence, and we forgot to make ourselves intelligent when we made ourselves sovereign. Education has spread, but intelligence is perpetually retarded by the fertility of the simple. A cynic remarked that "you mustn't enthrone ignorance just because there is so much of it." However, ignorance is not long enthroned, for it lends itself to manipulation by the forces that mold public opinion. It may be true, as Lincoln supposed, that "you can't fool all the people all the time," but you can fool enough of them to rule a large country.

Is democracy responsible for the current debasement of art? The debasement, of course, is not unquestioned; it is a matter of subjective judgment; and those of us who shudder at its excesses—its meaningless blotches of color, its collages of debris, its Babels of cacophony—are doubtless imprisoned in our past and dull to the courage of experiment. The producers of such nonsense are appealing not to the general public—which scorns them as lunatics, degenerates, or charlatans—but to gullible middle-class purchasers who are hypnotized by auctioneers and are thrilled by the new, however deformed. Democracy is responsible for this collapse only in the sense that it has not been able to develop standards and tastes to replace those with which aristocracies once kept the imagination and individualism of artists within the bounds of intelligible communication, the illumination of life, and the harmony of parts in a logical sequence and a coherent whole. If art now seems to lose itself in *bizarreries*, this is not only because it is vulgarized by mass suggestion or domination, but also because it has exhausted the possibilities of old schools and forms, and flounders for a time in the search for new patterns and styles, new rules and disciplines.

All deductions having been made, democracy has done less harm, and more good, than any other form of government. It gave to human existence a zest and camaraderie that outweighed its pitfalls and defects. It gave to thought and science and enterprise the freedom essential to their operation and growth. It broke down the walls of privilege and class, and in each generation it raised up ability from every rank and place. Under its stimulus Athens and Rome became the most creative cities in history, and America in two centuries has provided abundance for an unprecedentedly large proportion of its population. Democracy has now dedicated itself resolutely to the spread and lengthening of education, and to the maintenance of public health. If equality of educational opportunity can be established, democracy will be real and justified. For this is the vital truth beneath its catchwords: that though men cannot be equal, their access to education and opportunity can be made more nearly equal. The rights of man are not rights to office and power, but the rights of entry into every avenue that may nourish and test a man's fitness for office and power. A right is not a gift of God or nature but a privilege which it is good for the group that the individual should have.

In England and the United States, in Denmark, Norway, and Sweden, in Switzerland and Canada, democracy is today sounder than ever before. It has defended itself with courage and energy against the assaults of foreign dictatorship, and has not yielded to dictatorship at home. But if war continues to absorb and dominate it, or if the itch to rule the world requires a large military establishment and appropriation, the freedoms of democracy may one by one succumb to the discipline of arms and strife. If race or class war divides us into hostile camps, changing political argument into blind hate, one side or the other may overturn the hustings with the rule of the sword. If our economy of freedom fails to distribute wealth as ably as it has created it, the road to dictatorship will be open to any man

who can persuasively promise security to all; and a martial government, under whatever charming phrases, will engulf the democratic
world.

XI. History and War

War is one of the constants of history, and has not diminished with civilization or democracy. In the last 3,421 years of recorded history only 268 have seen no war. We have acknowledged war as at present the ultimate form of competition and natural selection in the human species. "*Polemos pater panton,*" said Heracleitus; war, or competition, is the father of all things, the potent source of ideas, inventions, institutions, and states. Peace is an unstable equilibrium, which can be preserved only by acknowledged supremacy or equal power.

The causes of war are the same as the causes of competition among individuals: acquisitiveness, pugnacity, and pride; the desire for food, land, materials, fuels, mastery. The state has our instincts without our restraints. The individual submits to restraints laid upon him by morals and laws, and agrees to replace combat with conference, because the state guarantees him basic protection in his life, property, and legal rights. The state itself acknowledges no substantial restraints, either because it is strong enough to defy any interference with its will or because there is no superstate to offer it basic protection, and no international law or moral code wielding effective force.

In the individual, pride gives added vigor in the competitions of life; in the state, nationalism gives added force in diplomacy and war. When the states of Europe freed themselves from papal overlordship and protection, each state encouraged nationalism as a supplement to its army and navy. If it foresaw conflict with any particular country it fomented, in its people, hatred of that country, and formulated catchwords to bring that hatred to a lethal point; meanwhile it stressed its love of peace.

This conscription of the soul to international phobia occurred only in the most elemental conflicts, and was seldom resorted to in Europe between the Religious Wars of the sixteenth century and the Wars of the French Revolution. During that interval the peoples of conflicting states were allowed to respect one another's achievements and civilization; Englishmen traveled safely in France while France was at war with England; and the French and Frederick the Great continued to admire each other while they fought each other in the Seven Years' War. In the seventeenth and eighteenth centuries war was a contest of aristocracies rather than of peoples. In the twentieth century the improvement of communication, transport, weapons, and means of indoctrination made war a struggle of peoples, involving civilians as well as combatants, and winning victory through the wholesale destruction of property and life. One war can now destroy the labor of centuries in building cities, creating art, and developing habits of civilization. In apologetic consolation war now promotes science and technology, whose deadly inventions, if they are not forgotten in universal destitution and barbarism, may later enlarge the material achievements of peace.

In every century the generals and the rulers (with rare exceptions like Ashoka and Augustus) have smiled at the philosophers' timid dislike of war. In the military interpretation of history war is the final arbiter, and is accepted as natural and necessary by all but cowards and simpletons. What but the victory of Charles Martel at

Tours (732) kept France and Spain from becoming Mohammedan? What would have happened to our classic heritage if it had not been protected by arms against Mongol and Tatar invasions? We laugh at generals who die in bed (forgetting that they are more valuable alive than dead), but we build statues to them when they turn back a Hitler or a Genghis Khan. It is pitiful (says the general) that so many young men die in battle, but more of them die in automobile accidents than in war, and many of them riot and rot for lack of discipline; they need an outlet for their combativeness, their adventurousness, their weariness with prosaic routine; if they must die sooner or later why not let them die for their country in the anesthesia of battle and the aura of glory? Even a philosopher, if he knows history, will admit that a long peace may fatally weaken the martial muscles of a nation. In the present inadequacy of international law and sentiment a nation must be ready at any moment to defend itself; and when its essential interests are involved it must be allowed to use any means it considers necessary to its survival. The Ten Commandments must be silent when self-preservation is at stake.

It is clear (continues the general) that the United States must assume today the task that Great Britain performed so well in the nineteenth century—the protection of Western civilization from external danger. Communist governments, armed with old birth rates and new weapons, have repeatedly proclaimed their resolve to destroy the economy and independence of non-Communist states. Young nations, longing for an Industrial Revolution to give them economic wealth and military power, are impressed by the rapid industrialization of Russia under governmental management; Western capitalism might be more productive in the end, but it seems slower in development; the new governors, eager to control the resources and manhood of their states, are a likely prey to Communist propaganda, infiltration, and subversion. Unless this spreading process is halted it is only a matter of time before nearly all Asia, Africa, and South America will be under Communist leadership, and Australia, New Zealand, North America, and Western Europe will be surrounded by enemies on every side. Imagine the effect of such a condition upon Japan, the Philippines, and India, and upon the powerful Communist Party of Italy; imagine the effect of a Communist victory in Italy upon the Communist movement in France. Great Britain, Scandinavia, the Netherlands, and West Germany would be left at the mercy of an overwhelmingly Communist Continent. Should North America, now at the height of its power, accept such a future as inevitable, withdraw within its frontiers, and let itself be encircled by hostile states controlling its access to materials and markets, and compelling it, like any besieged people, to imitate its enemies and establish governmental dictatorship over every phase of its once free and stimulating life? Should the leaders of America consider only the reluctance of this epicurean generation to face so great an issue, or should they consider also what future generations of Americans would wish that these leaders had done? Is it not wiser to resist at once, to carry the war to the enemy, to fight on foreign soil, to sacrifice, if it need be, a hundred thousand American lives and perhaps a million noncombatants, but to leave America free to live its own life in security and freedom? Is not such a farsighted policy fully in accord with the lessons of history?

The philosopher answers: Yes, and the devastating results will be in accord with history, except that they will be multiplied in proportion to the increased number and mobility of the engaged forces, and the unparalleled destructiveness of the weapons used. There is something greater than history. Somewhere, sometime, in the name of humanity, we must challenge a thousand evil precedents, and dare to apply the Golden Rule to nations, as the Buddhist King Ashoka did (262 B.C.),[64] or at least do what Augustus did when he bade Tiberius desist from further invasion of Germany (A.D. 9).[65] Let us refuse, at whatever cost to ourselves, to make a hundred Hiroshimas in China. "Magnanimity in politics," said Edmund Burke, "is not seldom the truest wisdom, and a great empire and little minds go ill together." [66] Imagine an American President saying to the leaders of China and Russia:

"If we should follow the usual course of history we should make war upon you for fear of what you may do a generation hence. Or we should follow the dismal precedent of the Holy Alliance of 1815, and dedicate our wealth and our soundest youth to suppressing any revolt against the existing order anywhere. But we are willing to try a new approach. We respect your peoples and your civilizations as among the most creative in history. We shall try to understand your feelings, and your desire to develop your own institutions without fear of attack. We must not allow our mutual fears to lead us into war, for the unparalleled murderousness of our weapons and yours brings into the situation an element unfamiliar to history. We propose to send representatives to join with yours in a persistent conference for the adjustment of our differences, the cessation of hostilities and subversion, and the reduction of our armaments. Wherever, outside our borders, we may find ourselves competing with you for the allegiance of a people, we are willing to submit to a full and fair election of the population concerned. Let us open our doors to each other, and organize cultural exchanges that will promote mutual appreciation and understanding. We are not afraid that your economic system will displace ours, nor need you fear that ours will displace yours; we believe that each system will learn from the other and be able to live with it in co-operation and peace. Perhaps each of us, while maintaining adequate defenses, can arrange nonaggression and nonsubversion pacts with other states, and from these accords a world order may take form within which each nation will remain sovereign and unique, limited only by agreements freely signed. We ask you to join us in this defiance of history, this resolve to extend courtesy and civilization to the relations among states. We pledge our honor before all mankind to enter into this venture in full sincerity and trust. If we lose in the historic gamble, the results could not be worse than those that we may expect from a continuation of traditional policies. If you and we succeed, we shall merit a place for centuries to come in the grateful memory of mankind."

The general smiles. "You have forgotten all the lessons of history," he says, "and all that nature of man which you described. Some conflicts are too fundamental to be resolved by negotiation; and during the prolonged negotiations (if history may be our guide) subversion would go on. A world order will come not by a gentlemen's agreement, but through so decisive a victory by one of the great powers that it will be able to dictate and enforce international law, as Rome did from Augustus to Aurelius. Such interludes of widespread peace are unnatural and exceptional; they will soon be ended by changes in the distribution of military power. You have told us that man is a competitive animal, that his states must be like himself, and that natural selection now operates on an international plane. States will unite in basic co-operation only when they are in common attacked from without. Perhaps we are now restlessly moving toward that higher plateau of competition; we may make contact with ambitious species on other planets or stars; soon thereafter there will be interplanetary war. Then, and only then, will we of this earth be one."

XII. Growth and Decay

We have defined civilization as "social order promoting cultural creation." [67] It is political order secured through custom, morals, and law, and economic order secured through a continuity of production and exchange; it is cultural creation through freedom and facilities for the origination, expression, testing, and fruition of ideas, letters, manners, and arts. It is an intricate and precarious web of human relationships, laboriously built and readily destroyed.

Why is it that history is littered with the ruins of civilizations, and seems to tell us, like Shelley's "Ozymandias," that death is the destiny of all? Are there any regularities, in this process of growth and decay, which may enable us to predict, from the course of past civilizations, the future of our own?

Certain imaginative spirits have thought so, even to predicting the future in detail. In his Fourth Eclogue Virgil announced that some day, the ingenuity of change having been exhausted, the whole universe, by design or accident, will fall into a condition precisely the same as in some forgotten antiquity, and will then repeat, by deterministic fatality and in every particular, all those events that had followed that condition before.

87

Alter erit tum Tiphys, et altera quae vehat Argo
delectos heroas; erunt etiam altera bella,
atque iterum ad Troiam magnus mittetur Achilles—

"there will then be another [prophet] Tiphys, and another Argo
will carry [Jason and other] beloved heroes; there will also be other
wars, and great Achilles will again be sent to Troy." [68] Friedrich
Nietzsche went insane with this vision of "eternal recurrence."
There is nothing so foolish but it can be found in the philosophers.

History repeats itself, but only in outline and in the large. We may
reasonably expect that in the future, as in the past, some new states
will rise, some old states will subside; that new civilizations will begin with pasture and agriculture, expand into commerce and industry, and luxuriate with finance; that thought (as Vico and Comte
argued) will pass, by and large, from supernatural to legendary to
naturalistic explanations; that new theories, inventions, discoveries,
and errors will agitate the intellectual currents; that new generations
will rebel against the old and pass from rebellion to conformity and
reaction; that experiments in morals will loosen tradition and
frighten its beneficiaries; and that the excitement of innovation will
be forgotten in the unconcern of time. History repeats itself in the
large because human nature changes with geological leisureliness,
and man is equipped to respond in stereotyped ways to frequently
occurring situations and stimuli like hunger, danger, and sex. But in a
developed and complex civilization individuals are more differenti-
ated and unique than in a primitive society, and many situations
contain novel circumstances requiring modifications of instinctive
response; custom recedes, reasoning spreads; the results are less pre-
dictable. There is no certainty that the future will repeat the past.
Every year is an adventure.

Some masterminds have sought to constrain the loose regularities
of history into majestic paradigms. The founder of French socialism,

Claude-Henri de Rouvroy, Comte de Saint-Simon (1760–1825), divided the past and the future into an alternation of "organic" and "critical" periods:

> The law of human development . . . reveals two distinct and alternative states of society: one, the organic, in which all human actions are classed, foreseen, and regulated by a general theory, and the purpose of social activity is clearly defined; the other, the critical, in which all community of thought, all communal action, all coordination have ceased, and the society is only an agglomeration of separate individuals in conflict with one another.
>
> Each of these states or conditions has occupied two periods of history. One organic period preceded that Greek era which we call the age of philosophy, but which we shall more justly call the age of criticism. Later a new doctrine arose, ran through different phases of elaboration and completion, and finally established its political power over Western civilization. The constitution of the Church began a new organic epoch, which ended in the fifteenth century, when the Reformers sounded the arrival of that age of criticism which has continued to our time. . . .
>
> In the organic ages all basic problems [theological, political, economic, moral] have received at least provisional solutions. But soon the progress achieved by the help of these solutions, and under the protection of the institutions realized through them, rendered them inadequate, and evoked novelties. Critical epochs—periods of debate, protest, . . . and transition, replaced the old mood with doubt, individualism, and indifference to the great problems. . . . In organic periods men are busy building; in critical periods they are busy destroying.[69]

Saint-Simon believed that the establishment of socialism would begin a new organic age of unified belief, organization, co-operation, and stability. If Communism should prove to be the triumphant new order of life Saint-Simon's analysis and prediction would be justified.

Oswald Spengler (1880–1936) varied Saint-Simon's scheme by dividing history into separate civilizations, each with an independent life span and trajectory composed of four seasons but essentially two

periods: one of centripetal organization unifying a culture in all its
phases into a unique, coherent, and artistic form; the other a period
of centrifugal disorganization in which creed and culture decompose
in division and criticism, and end in a chaos of individualism, skepticism, and artistic aberrations. Whereas Saint-Simon looked forward
to socialism as the new synthesis, Spengler (like Talleyrand) looked
backward to aristocracy as the age in which life and thought were
consistent and orderly and constituted a work of living art.

> For Western existence the distinction lies about the year 1800—on
> one side of that frontier, life in fullness and sureness of itself, formed
> by growth from within, in one great, uninterrupted evolution from
> Gothic childhood to Goethe and Napoleon; and on the other the
> autumnal, artificial, rootless life of our great cities, under forms fash-
> ioned by the intellect. . . . He who does not understand that this
> outcome is obligatory and insusceptible of modification must forgo
> all desire to comprehend history.[70]

On one point all are agreed: civilizations begin, flourish, decline,
and disappear—or linger on as stagnant pools left by once life-giving
streams. What are the causes of development, and what are the causes
of decay?

No student takes seriously the seventeenth-century notion that
states arose out of a "social contract" among individuals or between
the people and a ruler. Probably most states (i.e., societies politically
organized) took form through the conquest of one group by
another, and the establishment of a continuing force over the conquered by the conqueror; his decrees were their first laws; and these,
added to the customs of the people, created a new social order. Some
states of Latin America obviously began in this way. When the masters organized the work of their subjects to take advantage of some
physical boon (like the rivers of Egypt or Asia), economic prevision
and provision constituted another basis for civilization. A dangerous

tension between rulers and ruled might raise intellectual and emotional activity above the daily drift of primitive tribes. Further stimulation to growth could come from any challenging change in the surroundings,[71] such as external invasion or a continuing shortage of rain—challenges that might be met by military improvements or the construction of irrigation canals.

If we put the problem further back, and ask what determines whether a challenge will or will not be met, the answer is that this depends upon the presence or absence of initiative and of creative individuals with clarity of mind and energy of will (which is almost a definition of genius), capable of effective responses to new situations (which is almost a definition of intelligence). If we ask what makes a creative individual, we are thrown back from history to psychology and biology—to the influence of environment and the gamble and secret of the chromosomes. In any case a challenge successfully met (as by the United States in 1917, 1933, and 1941), if it does not exhaust the victor (like England in 1945), raises the temper and level of a nation, and makes it abler to meet further challenges.

If these are the sources of growth, what are the causes of decay? Shall we suppose, with Spengler and many others, that each civilization is an organism, naturally and yet mysteriously endowed with the power of development and the fatality of death? It is tempting to explain the behavior of groups through analogy with physiology or physics, and to ascribe the deterioration of a society to some inherent limit in its loan and tenure of life, or some irreparable running down of internal force. Such analogies may offer provisional illumination, as when we compare the association of individuals with an aggregation of cells, or the circulation of money from banker back to banker with the systole and diastole of the heart. But a group is no organism physically added to its constituent individuals; it has no brain or stomach of its own; it must think or feel with the brains or nerves of its members. When the group or a civilization declines, it is through no mystic limitation of a corporate life, but through the failure of its political or intellectual leaders to meet the challenges of change.

The challenges may come from a dozen sources, and may by repetition or combination rise to a destructive intensity. Rainfall or oases may fail and leave the earth parched to sterility. The soil may be exhausted by incompetent husbandry or improvident usage. The replacement of free with slave labor may reduce the incentives to production, leaving lands untilled and cities unfed. A change in the instruments or routes of trade—as by the conquest of the ocean or the air—may leave old centers of civilization becalmed and decadent, like Pisa or Venice after 1492. Taxes may mount to the point of discouraging capital investment and productive stimulus. Foreign markets and materials may be lost to more enterprising competition; excess of imports over exports may drain precious metal from domestic reserves. The concentration of wealth may disrupt the nation in class or race war. The concentration of population and poverty in great cities may compel a government to choose between enfeebling the economy with a dole and running the risk of riot and revolution.

Since inequality grows in an expanding economy, a society may find itself divided between a cultured minority and a majority of men and women too unfortunate by nature or circumstance to inherit or develop standards of excellence and taste. As this majority grows it acts as a cultural drag upon the minority; its ways of speech, dress, recreation, feeling, judgment, and thought spread upward, and internal barbarization by the majority is part of the price that the minority pays for its control of educational and economic opportunity.

As education spreads, theologies lose credence, and receive an external conformity without influence upon conduct or hope. Life and ideas become increasingly secular, ignoring supernatural explanations and fears. The moral code loses aura and force as its human origin is revealed, and as divine surveillance and sanctions are removed. In ancient Greece the philosophers destroyed the old faith among the educated classes; in many nations of modern Europe the philosophers achieved similar results. Protagoras became Voltaire, Diogenes Rousseau, Democritus Hobbes, Plato Kant, Thrasymachus Nietzsche, Aristotle Spencer, Epicurus Diderot. In antiquity and modernity alike, analytical thought dissolved the religion that had buttressed the moral code. New religions came, but they were divorced from the ruling classes, and gave no service to the state. An age of weary skepticism and epicureanism followed the triumph of rationalism over mythology in the last century before Christianity, and follows a similar victory today in the first century after Christianity.

Caught in the relaxing interval between one moral code and the next, an unmoored generation surrenders itself to luxury, corruption, and a restless disorder of family and morals, in all but a remnant clinging desperately to old restraints and ways. Few souls feel any longer that "it is beautiful and honorable to die for one's country." A failure of leadership may allow a state to weaken itself with internal strife. At the end of the process a decisive defeat in war may bring a final blow, or barbarian invasion from without may combine with barbarism welling up from within to bring the civilization to a close.

Is this a depressing picture? Not quite. Life has no inherent claim to eternity, whether in individuals or in states. Death is natural, and if it comes in due time it is forgivable and useful, and the mature mind will take no offense from its coming. But do civilizations die? Again, not quite. Greek civilization is not really dead; only its frame is gone and its habitat has changed and spread; it survives in the memory of the race, and in such abundance that no one life, however full and long, could absorb it all. Homer has more readers now than in his own day and land. The Greek poets and philosophers are in every library and college; at this moment Plato is being studied by a hundred thousand discoverers of the "dear delight" of philosophy overspreading life with understanding thought. This selective survival of creative minds is the most real and beneficent of immortalities.

Nations die. Old regions grow arid, or suffer other change. Resilient man picks up his tools and his arts, and moves on, taking his memories with him. If education has deepened and broadened those memories, civilization migrates with him, and builds somewhere another home. In the new land he need not begin entirely anew, nor make his way without friendly aid; communication and transport bind him, as in a nourishing placenta, with his mother country. Rome imported Greek civilization and transmitted it to Western Europe; America profited from European civilization and prepares to pass it on, with a technique of transmission never equaled before.

Civilizations are the generations of the racial soul. As life overrides death with reproduction, so an aging culture hands its patrimony down to its heirs across the years and the seas. Even as these lines are being written, commerce and print, wires and waves and invisible Mercuries of the air are binding nations and civilizations together, preserving for all what each has given to the heritage of mankind.

XIII . Is Progress Real?[72]

Against this panorama of nations, morals, and religions rising and falling, the idea of progress finds itself in dubious shape. Is it only the vain and traditional boast of each "modern" generation? Since we have admitted no substantial change in man's nature during historic times, all technological advances will have to be written off as merely new means of achieving old ends—the acquisition of goods, the pursuit of one sex by the other (or by the same), the overcoming of competition, the fighting of wars. One of the discouraging discoveries of our disillusioning century is that science is neutral: it will kill for us as readily as it will heal, and will destroy for us more readily than it can build. How inadequate now seems the proud motto of Francis Bacon, "Knowledge is power"! Sometimes we feel that the Middle Ages and the Renaissance, which stressed mythology and art rather than science and power, may have been wiser than we, who repeatedly enlarge our instrumentalities without improving our purposes.

Our progress in science and technique has involved some tincture of evil with good. Our comforts and conveniences may have weakened our physical stamina and our moral fiber. We have immensely

developed our means of locomotion, but some of us use them to facilitate crime and to kill our fellow men or ourselves. We double, triple,
centuple our speed, but we shatter our nerves in the process, and are
the same trousered apes at two thousand miles an hour as when we
had legs. We applaud the cures and incisions of modern medicine if
they bring no side effects worse than the malady; we appreciate the
assiduity of our physicians in their mad race with the resilience of
microbes and the inventiveness of disease; we are grateful for the
added years that medical science gives us if they are not a burden-
some prolongation of illness, disability, and gloom. We have multiplied a hundred times our ability to learn and report the events of the
day and the planet, but at times we envy our ancestors, whose peace
was only gently disturbed by the news of their village. We have
laudably bettered the conditions of life for skilled workingmen and
the middle class, but we have allowed our cities to fester with dark
ghettos and slimy slums.

We frolic in our emancipation from theology, but have we developed a natural ethic—a moral code independent of religion—strong
enough to keep our instincts of acquisition, pugnacity, and sex from
debasing our civilization into a mire of greed, crime, and promis-
cuity? Have we really outgrown intolerance, or merely transferred
it from religious to national, ideological, or racial hostilities? Are our
manners better than before, or worse? "Manners," said a nineteenth-
century traveler, "get regularly worse as you go from the East to
the West; it is bad in Asia, not so good in Europe, and altogether bad
in the western states of America";[73] and now the East imitates the
West. Have our laws offered the criminal too much protection
against society and the state? Have we given ourselves more freedom
than our intelligence can digest? Or are we nearing such moral and
social disorder that frightened parents will run back to Mother
Church and beg her to discipline their children, at whatever cost to

intellectual liberty? Has all the progress of philosophy since Descartes been a mistake through its failure to recognize the role of myth in the consolation and control of man? "He that increaseth knowledge increaseth sorrow, and in much wisdom is much grief." [74]

Has there been any progress at all in philosophy since Confucius? Or in literature since Aeschylus? Are we sure that our music, with its complex forms and powerful orchestras, is more profound than Palestrina, or more musical and inspiring than the monodic airs that medieval Arabs sang to the strumming of their simple instruments? (Edward Lane said of the Cairo musicians, "I have been more charmed with their songs . . . than with any other music that I have ever enjoyed." [75]) How does our contemporary architecture— bold, original, and impressive as it is—compare with the temples of ancient Egypt or Greece, or our sculpture with the statues of Chephren and Hermes, or our bas-reliefs with those of Persepolis or the Parthenon, or our paintings with those of the van Eycks or Holbein? If "the replacement of chaos with order is the essence of art and civilization," [76] is contemporary painting in America and Western Europe the replacement of order with chaos, and a vivid symbol of our civilization's relapse into confused and structureless decay?

History is so indifferently rich that a case for almost any conclusion from it can be made by a selection of instances. Choosing our evidence with a brighter bias, we might evolve some more comforting reflections. But perhaps we should first define what progress means to us. If it means increase in happiness its case is lost almost at first sight. Our capacity for fretting is endless, and no matter how many difficulties we surmount, how many ideals we realize, we shall always find an excuse for being magnificently miserable; there is a stealthy pleasure in rejecting mankind or the universe as unworthy of our approval. It seems silly to define progress in terms that would make the average child a higher, more advanced product of life than the adult or the sage—for certainly the child is the happiest of the three. Is a more objective definition possible? We shall here define progress as the increasing control of the environment by life. It is a test that may hold for the lowliest organism as well as for man.

We must not demand of progress that it should be continuous or universal. Obviously there are retrogressions, just as there are periods of failure, fatigue, and rest in a developing individual; if the present stage is an advance in control of the environment, progress is real. We may presume that at almost any time in history some nations were progressing and some were declining, as Russia progresses and England loses ground today. The same nation may be progressing in one field of human activity and retrogressing in another, as America is now progressing in technology and receding in the graphic arts. If we find that the type of genius prevalent in young countries like America and Australia tends to the practical, inventive, scientific, executive kinds rather than to the painter of pictures or poems, the carver of statues or words, we must understand that each age and place needs and elicits some types of ability rather than others in its pursuit of environmental control. We should not compare the work of one land and time with the winnowed best of all the collected past. Our problem is whether the average man has increased his ability to control the conditions of his life.

If we take a long-range view and compare our modern existence, precarious, chaotic, and murderous as it is, with the ignorance, superstition, violence, and diseases of primitive peoples, we do not come off quite forlorn. The lowliest strata in civilized states may still differ only slightly from barbarians, but above those levels thousands, millions have reached mental and moral levels rarely found among primitive men. Under the complex strains of city life we sometimes take imaginative refuge in the supposed simplicity of pre-civilized ways; but in our less romantic moments we know that this is a flight reaction from our actual tasks, and that the idolizing of savages, like many other young moods, is an impatient expression of adolescent maladaptation, of conscious ability not yet matured and comfortably placed. The "friendly and flowing savage" would be delightful but for his scalpel, his insects, and his dirt. A study of surviving primitive tribes reveals their high rate of infantile mortality, their short tenure of life, their lesser stamina and speed, their greater susceptibility to disease.[77] If the prolongation of life indicates better control of the environment, then the tables of mortality proclaim the advance of man, for longevity in European and American whites has tripled in the last three centuries. Some time ago a convention of morticians discussed the danger threatening their industry from the increasing tardiness of men in keeping their rendezvous with death.[78] But if undertakers are miserable progress is real.

In the debate between ancients and moderns it is not at all clear that the ancients carry off the prize. Shall we count it a trivial achievement that famine has been eliminated in modern states, and that one country can now grow enough food to overfeed itself and yet send hundreds of millions of bushels of wheat to nations in need? Are we ready to scuttle the science that has so diminished superstition, obscurantism, and religious intolerance, or the technology that has spread food, home ownership, comfort, education, and leisure beyond any precedent? Would we really prefer the Athenian agora or the Roman comitia to the British Parliament or the United States Congress, or be content under a narrow franchise like Attica's, or the selection of rulers by a praetorian guard? Would we rather have lived under the laws of the Athenian Republic or the Roman Empire than under constitutions that give us habeas corpus, trial by jury, religious and intellectual freedom, and the emancipation of women? Are our morals, lax though they are, worse than those of the ambisexual Alcibiades, or has any American President imitated Pericles, who lived with a learned courtesan? Are we ashamed of our great universities, our many publishing houses, our bountiful public libraries? There were great dramatists in Athens, but was any greater than Shakespeare, and was Aristophanes as profound and humane as Molière? Was the oratory of Demosthenes, Isocrates, and Aeschines superior to that of Chatham, Burke, and Sheridan? Shall we place Gibbon below Herodotus or Thucydides? Is there anything in ancient prose fiction comparable to the scope and depth of the modern novel? We may grant the superiority of the ancients in art, though some of us might still prefer Notre Dame de Paris to the Parthenon. If the Founding Fathers of the United States could return to America, or Fox and Bentham to England, or Voltaire and Diderot to France, would they not reproach us as ingrates for our blindness to our good fortune in living today and not yesterday—not even under Pericles or Augustus?

We should not be greatly disturbed by the probability that our civilization will die like any other. As Frederick asked his retreating troops at Kolin, "Would you live forever?" [79] Perhaps it is desirable that life should take fresh forms, that new civilizations and centers should have their turn. Meanwhile the effort to meet the challenge of the rising East may reinvigorate the West.

We have said that a great civilization does not entirely die—*non omnis moritur*. Some precious achievements have survived all the vicissitudes of rising and falling states: the making of fire and light, of the wheel and other basic tools; language, writing, art, and song; agriculture, the family, and parental care; social organization, morality, and charity; and the use of teaching to transmit the lore of the family and the race. These are the elements of civilization, and they have been tenaciously maintained through the perilous passage from one civilization to the next. They are the connective tissue of human history.

If education is the transmission of civilization, we are unquestionably progressing. Civilization is not inherited; it has to be learned and earned by each generation anew; if the transmission should be interrupted for one century, civilization would die, and we should be savages again. So our finest contemporary achievement is our unprecedented expenditure of wealth and toil in the provision of higher education for all. Once colleges were luxuries, designed for the male half of the leisure class; today universities are so numerous that he who runs may become a Ph.D. We may not have excelled the selected geniuses of antiquity, but we have raised the level and average of knowledge beyond any age in history.

None but a child will complain that our teachers have not yet eradicated the errors and superstitions of ten thousand years. The great experiment has just begun, and it may yet be defeated by the high birth rate of unwilling or indoctrinated ignorance. But what would be the full fruitage of instruction if every child should be schooled till at least his twentieth year, and should find free access to the universities, libraries, and museums that harbor and offer the intellectual and artistic treasures of the race? Consider education not as the painful accumulation of facts and dates and reigns, nor merely the necessary preparation of the individual to earn his keep in the world, but as the transmission of our mental, moral, technical, and aesthetic heritage as fully as possible to as many as possible, for the enlargement of man's understanding, control, embellishment, and enjoyment of life.

The heritage that we can now more fully transmit is richer than ever before. It is richer than that of Pericles, for it includes all the Greek flowering that followed him; richer than Leonardo's, for it includes him and the Italian Renaissance; richer than Voltaire's, for it embraces all the French Enlightenment and its ecumenical dissemination. If progress is real despite our whining, it is not because we are born any healthier, better, or wiser than infants were in the past, but because we are born to a richer heritage, born on a higher level of that pedestal which the accumulation of knowledge and art raises as the ground and support of our being. The heritage rises, and man rises in proportion as he receives it.

History is, above all else, the creation and recording of that heritage; progress is its increasing abundance, preservation, transmission, and use. To those of us who study history not merely as a warning reminder of man's follies and crimes, but also as an encouraging remembrance of generative souls, the past ceases to be a depressing chamber of horrors; it becomes a celestial city, a spacious country of the mind, wherein a thousand saints, statesmen, inventors, scientists, poets, artists, musicians, lovers, and philosophers still live and speak, teach and carve and sing. The historian will not mourn because he can see no meaning in human existence except that which man puts into it; let it be our pride that we ourselves may put meaning into our lives, and sometimes a significance that transcends death. If a man is fortunate he will, before he dies, gather up as much as he can of his civilized heritage and transmit it to his children. And to his final breath he will be grateful for this inexhaustible legacy, knowing that it is our nourishing mother and our lasting life.

Guide to Books

mentioned in the Notes

ARISTOTLE, *Politics*. Everyman's Library.

BAGEHOT, WALTER, *Physics and Politics*. Boston, 1956.

CARTER, THOMAS F., *The Invention of Printing in China and Its Spread Westward*. New York, 1925.

COXE, WILLIAM, *History of the House of Austria*, 3v. London, 1847.

DURANT, WILL, *The Mansions of Philosophy*. New York, 1929.

DURANT, WILL and ARIEL, *The Story of Civilization*:

    I. *Our Oriental Heritage*. New York, 1935.

    II. *The Life of Greece*. New York, 1939.

    III. *Caesar and Christ*. New York, 1944.

    IV. *The Age of Faith*. New York, 1950.

    V. *The Renaissance*. New York, 1953.

    VI. *The Reformation*. New York, 1957.

    VII. *The Age of Reason Begins*. New York, 1961.

    VIII. *The Age of Louis XIV*. New York, 1963.

    IX. *The Age of Voltaire*. New York, 1965.

    X. *Rousseau and Revolution*. New York, 1967.

Encyclopaedia Britannica, 1966 edition.

GIBBON, EDWARD, *The Decline and Fall of the Roman Empire*, ed. Milman, 6v. New York: Nottingham Society, n.d.

GOBINEAU, J. A. DE, *The Inequality of Human Races*. London, 1915.

GOMME, A. W., *The Population of Athens in the Fifth and Fourth Centuries B.C.* Oxford, 1933.

GOWEN, H. H., AND HALL, JOSEF, *Outline History of China*. New York, 1927.

GRANET, MARCEL, *Chinese Civilization*. New York, 1930.

ISOCRATES, *Works*. Loeb Library.

KAUTSKY, KARL, *Communism in Central Europe in the Time of the Reformation*. London, 1897.

LANE, EDWARD, *Manners and Customs of the Modern Egyptians*, 2v. London, 1846.

LEMAÎTRE, JULES, *Jean Jacques Rousseau*. New York, 1907.

PASCAL, BLAISE, *Pensées*. Everyman's Library.

PAUL-LOUIS, *Ancient Rome at Work*. London, 1927.

PLATO, *Dialogues*, tr. Jowett, 4v. New York: Jefferson Press, n.d.

PLUTARCH, *Lives*, 3v. Everyman's Library.

RENAN, ERNEST, *The Apostles*. London: Methuen, n.d.

———, *Marc Aurèle*. Paris: Calman-Lévy, n.d.

SÉDILLOT, RENÉ, *L'Histoire n'a pas de sens*. Paris, 1965.

SEEBOHM, FREDERICK, *The Age of Johnson*. London, 1899.

SIEGFRIED, ANDRÉ, *America Comes of Age*. New York, 1927.

SPENGLER, OSWALD, *The Decline of the West*, 2v. New York, 1927.

THUCYDIDES, *History of the Peloponnesian War*. Everyman's Library.

TODD, A. J., *Theories of Social Progress*. New York, 1934.

TOYNBEE, ARNOLD J., *A Study of History*, 10v. London, 1934f.

Notes

CHAPTER I

1. Sédillot, René, *L'Histoire n'a pas de sens.*
2. Durant, *Our Oriental Heritage,* 12.
3. *Age of Faith,* 979.
4. Sédillot, 167.
5. *The Reformation, viii.*
6. *The Age of Reason Begins,* 267.

CHAPTER II

7. Pascal, *Pensées,* No. 347.
8. Plato, *Phaedo,* No. 109.

CHAPTER III

9. *Caesar and Christ,* 193, 223, 666.

CHAPTER IV

10. Gobineau, *Inequality of Human Races, xv,* 210.
11. *Ibid.,* 211.
12. *Ibid.,* 36-7.
13. In Todd, A. J., *Theories of Social Progress,* 276.
14. See *Our Oriental Heritage,* 934-38.

CHAPTER VI

15. *Caesar and Christ,* 211.
16. *The Renaissance,* 576.

17. *Our Oriental Heritage,* 275.
18. *The Reformation,* 761.
19. *The Age of Reason Begins,* 394.
20. *The Age of Voltaire,* 64.
21. *Our Oriental Heritage,* 265.
22. *The Reformation,* 763.
23. *The Age of Voltaire,* 487.
24. Gibbon, Edward, *Decline and Fall of the Roman Empire,* I, 314.

CHAPTER VII

25. *Caesar and Christ,* 296-97.
26. *The Age of Faith,* 525-26.
27. Plato, *Laws,* No. 948.
28. *Our Oriental Heritage,* 205-13.
29. *Ibid.,* 416-19, 434, 504.
30. Renan, *The Apostles, xxxiii.*
31. Lemaître, *Jean Jacques Rousseau,* 9.
32. Durant, *The Mansions of Philosophy,* 568.

CHAPTER VIII

33. *The Reformation,* 752.
34. *The Age of Louis XIV,* 720.
35. Plutarch, *Life of Solon.*
36. *The Life of Greece,* 112-18.
37. Plutarch, *Tiberius Gracchus.*
38. *Caesar and Christ,* 111-22, 142-44, 180-208.

CHAPTER IX

39. *Encyclopaedia Britannica*, II, 962b.
40. *Our Oriental Heritage*, 231. We have revised the date there given for Hammurabi.
41. *The Life of Greece*, 587–92.
42. Paul-Louis, *Ancient Rome at Work*, 283–85.
43. *Caesar and Christ*, 641f.
44. Szuma Ch'ien in Granet, Marcel, *Chinese Civilization*, 113.
45. *Ibid.*
46. *Our Oriental Heritage*, 700f. The dates there given are being revised for a new edition.
47. Gowen and Hall, *Outline History of China*, 142.
48. In Carter, Thomas, *The Invention of Printing in China and Its Spread Westward*, 183.
49. *Our Oriental Heritage*, 724–26.
50. *The Age of Reason Begins*, 249–51.
51. Kautsky, Karl, *Communism in Central Europe in the Time of the Reformation*, 121, 130.
52. *The Reformation*, 383, 391, 398–401.

CHAPTER X

53. Renan, *Marc Aurèle*, 479.
54. Gibbon, *Decline and Fall*, I, 31.
55. Gomme, A. W., *The Population of Athens in the Fifth and Fourth Centuries B.C.*, 21, 26, 47; *Life of Greece*, 254.
56. Thucydides, *Peloponnesian War*, iii 10; *Life of Greece*, 284.
57. Plato, *The Republic*, Nos. 560–64.

58. *Ibid.*, No. 422.
59. Aristotle, *Politics,* No. 1310.
60. Isocrates, *Works,* "Archidamus," No. 67.
61. This paragraph has been copied from *The Life of Greece*, 464–66.
62. *Caesar and Christ*, 128–30.
63. *Ibid.*

CHAPTER XI

64. *Our Oriental Heritage*, 446.
65. *Caesar and Christ*, 218.
66. In Seebohm, *The Age of Johnson*, xiii.

CHAPTER XII

67. *Our Oriental Heritage*, 1.
68. See *The Mansions of Philosophy*, 355; Toynbee, *A Study of History*, IV, 27f.
69. Quoted from Bazard's *Exposition de la doctrine Saint-Simonienne*, in Toynbee, I, 199.
70. Spengler, *Decline of the West*, I, 353, 90, 38.
71. This is the initial theory of Toynbee's *Study of History*, I, 271f.

CHAPTER XIII

72. This section appropriates some passages from an essay on the same subject in *The Mansions of Philosophy*.
73. Anon. in Bagehot, *Physics and Politics*, 110.
74. Ecclesiastes, i, 18.

75. Lane, Edward, *Manners and Customs of the Modern Egyptians*, II, 66.

76. *Our Oriental Heritage*, 237.

77. Todd, *Theories of Social Progress*, 135.

78. Siegfried, André, *America Comes of Age*, 176.

79. *Rousseau and Revolution*, Ch. II, Sec. iii, William Coxe, *History of the House of Austria*, III, 379.

Index

Dates in parentheses following a name are of birth and death except when preceded by *r*., when they indicate duration of reign for popes and rulers of states. A single date preceded by *fl*. denotes a *floruit*. A footnote is indicated by an asterisk. All dates are A.D. unless otherwise noted.

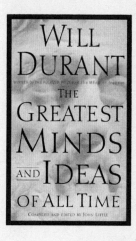
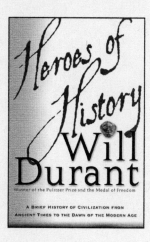